D1564161

PERSONAL ACCOUNT

PERSONAL ACCOUNT

25 TALES ABOUT
LEADERSHIP, LEARNING,
AND LEGACY FROM
A LIFETIME AT
BANK OF MONTREAL

TONY COMPER

with Bruce Dowbiggin

Published by ECW Press
665 Gerrard Street East
Toronto, Ontario, Canada M4M 1Y2
416-694-3348 / info@ecwpress.com

Cover design: Tania Craan
Front cover photograph by Yuula Benivolski
Author photo: Canwest News Service

LIBRARY AND ARCHIVES CANADA CATALOGUING IN
PUBLICATION

Title: Personal account : 25 tales about leadership, learning, and
legacy from a lifetime at Bank of Montreal / Tony Comper ;
with Bruce Dowbiggin.

Names: Comper, Tony, author. | Dowbiggin, Bruce, author.

Description: Includes index.

Identifiers: Canadiana (print) 20200266020 | Canadiana
(ebook) 2020026608X

ISBN 978-1-77041-517-1 (hardcover)
ISBN 978-1-77305-574-9 (PDF)
ISBN 978-1-77305-573-2 (ePUB)

Subjects: LCSH: Comper, Tony. | LCSH: Bank of Montreal—
Employees—Biography. | LCSH: Chief executive officers—
Canada—Biography. | LCSH: Bank management—Canada.
| LCSH: Banks and banking—Canada. | LCSH: Success in
business. | LCGFT: Autobiographies.

Classification: LCC HG2708.M66 C66 2020
DDC 332.1092—dc23

The publication of *Personal Account* is funded in part by the Government of Canada. *Ce livre est financé en partie par le gouvernement du Canada*. We also acknowledge the contribution of the Government of Ontario through Ontario Creates for the marketing of this book.

PRINTED AND BOUND IN CANADA

PRINTING: FRIESENS   5   4   3   2   1

To my dear friends Carol and Bruce,
without whom this memoir never would have happened.

And to the memory of my beloved Liz,
who shared each and every tale and inspired many of them.

The life so brief, the art so long in the learning, the attempt so hard, the conquest so sharp, the fearful joy that ever slips away so quickly — by all this I mean love, which so sorely astounds my feeling with its wondrous operation, that when I think upon it I scarce know whether I wake or sleep.

— GEOFFREY CHAUCER, *Parliament of Fowls*

CONTENTS

FOREWORD

By Larry Tanenbaum OC

Tony Comper is a visionary and a futurist. He doesn't just have a vision — he has the gift of being able to execute, to create reality out of that vision. This is a very special and rare gift.

He and his wife Liz had a home on Yonge near Summerhill. There was a park behind it, and I remember the story that he and Liz would look out their window and see these young kids playing soccer on the field that was near their home. They enjoyed watching those kids play the game and they knew that one day they would like to become more involved in soccer.

A number of years later, I came to Tony with the idea of BMO participating as our major corporate partner in Toronto FC and told him about the soccer pitch we were building. Tony supported our idea and our vision and brought BMO on board as our major corporate sponsor. Today, Toronto FC play at BMO Field and proudly display the BMO logo on their jerseys.

Tony deserves much of the credit for supporting the idea that BMO should be a part of Major League Soccer. I remember when we introduced Toronto FC to the city. The Bank had created soccer balls with the BMO logo on them and they were being given away at BMO branches throughout the city. It caused a great deal of excitement in many of our communities around the BMO bank branches, as soccer is a number-one sport among many first- and second-generation Canadian immigrants.

Tony knew this was an opportunity for BMO to develop a higher profile within the communities they served. It wasn't just about putting BMO's name on jerseys and on the stadium — their support had engaged people who were very involved with and truly passionate about the game, and this has been great for our team, our city and for Major League Soccer. As a footnote, BMO has also supported soccer at the grassroots level for years, and there are now over 800,000 kids registered in leagues and playing soccer in Canada today.

Our organization worked very closely with the people at BMO to develop the right branding. Toronto FC has gone on to win the MLS Cup, Supporters' Shield and the Canadian Championship, and BMO has been there through all of it because of Tony's vision and desire that his bank should be a part of the beautiful game.

We now have three MLS teams in Canada: Montreal, Vancouver and Toronto. Toronto FC has the distinction of being first, and BMO's endorsement has provided the very strong foundation from which we have grown our fan base and developed our team. We can credit them with helping us succeed in a very big way, where various teams had not been able to do so.

In addition to his vision and business acumen, Tony is a very special guy, and with his wife, Liz, has given a tremendous amount to the community. They were a great couple and had such a wonderful relationship. They were two different characters, but they balanced each other beautifully. Liz was the life of the party. She was no shrinking violet, but in a very nice way. She never pushed herself on people. She was a very genuine woman. Together and separately they supported many philanthropic endeavours, but it wasn't only the money they gave — it was the time, the energy and enthusiasm they devoted to their charitable causes, none more so than the program they founded, Fighting Antisemitism Together (FAST), which you will read more about later in the book.

Larry Tanenbaum is the chairman of, and a major shareholder in, Maple Leaf Sports & Entertainment, as well as the co-owner of the 2019 NBA champion Toronto Raptors, Toronto Maple Leafs, Toronto Argonauts and MLS champions Toronto FC. Larry is a highly successful entrepreneur and philanthropist. BMO partnered with Larry in support of Toronto FC and BMO Field in Toronto.

CHAPTER 1

Festina Lente: Make Haste Slowly

*Now I pray to all those who hear or read this little
treatise . . . if there should be anything that displeases
them, I pray them also that they attribute it to
the fault of my ignorance, and not to my will, which
would most eagerly have said better if I had had knowledge.
For our book says, all that is written is for our
teaching and that is my intention.*
— GEOFFREY CHAUCER, *The Canterbury Tales*

The day in February 1999 when I was handed the responsibility as
Chief Executive Officer of BMO following Matthew Barrett, I soon
understood I had accepted more than a job. I had inherited a serious
situation with no time to learn the ropes. The government had just
turned down a proposed merger between Bank of Montreal and Royal
Bank of Canada. People wanted answers from me on where we would go
next. They wanted to know what answers I might have for the future of
BMO. In the face of this urgency, I just repeated my mantra: *festina lente*.
Make haste slowly. Whatever moves I made, they would not be rushed.
It might have been easy to act quickly in my new job, to impress people
with speed. But I knew there was much time ahead to get it right.

As I looked at the challenges of a new millennium ahead, I was also
looking backward. That day, I received a trust begun in 1817 by people
who knew Canada was different and needed to be served differently
if it were to achieve its destiny in the world. The way to achieve that

destiny was through a stable banking system that reflected not London, not New York, but Canada. The group that launched the enterprise has succeeded, probably beyond its wildest dreams. Their boldness and courage were as true in 1999 as they were in 1817. Having said that, I saw that for me to succeed I had to be myself, not imitate the past.

I also knew the responsibility that trust carried. Although I might move among prime ministers and business tycoons, I was also walking with the customer whose life was invested with us. It wasn't just our employees and shareholders to whom I owed a debt of service. While the public image of banks is often cold and impersonal, to me the reality is the absolute opposite — the public we serve is a choir of many voices with hopes and dreams. The balance between creating opportunity for customers while protecting their wealth is the other great trust I was handed. Quite something for a kid who once planned to be an English professor teaching Chaucer.

As I said in my farewell speech in 2007, I had started working at Bank of Montreal in the glorious we-can-do-anything summer of 1967. I chose this professional life, because I knew then that BMO was an honourable place, that I would never have to mumble the answer when asked where I worked or feel the need to mount a defence of my bank. From my time working summers there as a student, I knew it was filled with good, decent, salt-of-the-earth people who had no stronger motive in their working life than the success of their customers — a quality I believe endures to this day. My summer job turned into a lifelong career at the Bank of Montreal, full of rich experiences. I learned a lot of leadership wisdom along the way, some of which I'll share in the pages of this book.

The most obvious reason I stayed, I suppose, was the culture and leadership of the place. I had a succession of really good jobs that kept getting better all the time — up to and including the privilege of leading one of the world's great financial institutions. My working life at the Bank of Montreal was blessed by great mentors and patrons (I say this in the clear understanding that heritage and gender were often on my side). The deeper, more abiding reason I hung around so long is that I often was surrounded by just the kind of people I wanted to be around, from the gentle folks at my local branch back in the mid-'60s to the management team and boards of directors at the turn of the twenty-first century.

I'm often asked, what are the defining issues that have made BMO/ Bank of Montreal unique? I'll address this question in detail in the chapters to come, but, briefly, I'd identify three key factors: First, our risk management concept, established under CEO William Mulholland in the 1980s, sets us apart. It has allowed us to significantly outperform the competition since that time. I like to think of us as the Porsche of financial institutions.

The second factor that defined us, closely related to the first, would be diversification. As I'll discuss later, our risk-management strategy prevented us from concentrating our holdings in a limited number of asset classes and ensured that we didn't have all our eggs in too few baskets. It allowed us to buy up banks domestically and globally that hadn't themselves diversified but were complementary to our business, while also establishing a toehold in communities and institutions across the country before our competition.

The third defining factor would be productivity. While you can't always control revenues, you can control costs. By getting people to buy into productivity, as we did in the days after the non-merger with the Royal Bank, the Bank has consistently managed our exposure while staying competitive.

I've always understood that nothing in banking, or life, stands still. As great as the founders' legacy was, it always needs to evolve. I know that from my own experience that has spanned five decades of banking, which has evolved from handwritten account statements to depositing cheques via cell phone. The Bank had to change with me, and I recognized that others would someday change my work.

During my tenure as CEO, constant revolutions and evolutions in the world altered the very fabric of business. As I said in my 2007 retirement address, globalization (which in my opinion has been an unqualified success despite some recent challenges) is probably the first that leaps to mind. It has changed the way we do business — and the way we *think* about business — so profoundly that even the word "profoundly" only begins to describe it.

The second was the technology revolution that made the customer supreme. From cross-border banking to real-time transactions to negotiating mortgages in your kitchen, the customer today controls the process in a way that would baffle my father, who worked in the financial world his whole business career. Or my grandmother, for that matter, who would take her bank book to Bank of Montreal branches to have it updated by hand.

The third of the three great turn-of-the-century revolutions has, in the long run, been almost as world-bending as the other two: corporate responsibility has gone from a dubious proposition, at best, to a core value and operating principle for most of the post-industrial world, and from a traditional cost centre to a competitive edge on the bottom line. I hope I've done them all the justice they deserve.

The triumphs, trials and tribulations of my forty years at BMO, both professional and personal, have given me a window into the soul of the nation and into my own perspective on Canada. One of my good friends likes to remind me of my own observation that at this stage of my life I have only twenty-five stories that have a lot of meaning to me. I'm bound to repeat them, as my father used to do his own. So when she brought up the idea of compiling a memoir of my experiences and lessons learned for the benefit of my successors, she said, "Why don't you just recount your experiences in the twenty-five stories that you always say sum up your life experiences?" Eureka! Her suggestion stuck, and here we are.

I then had to decide what I was going to share and who my audience would be. I knew I didn't want it to be simply a book about banking in Canada — it had to go beyond the predictable numbers and facts to describe the spirit that moved me. I want this memoir to be a gift to the colleagues and friends I made along the way at BMO and in the industry itself. But I want it also to impart some wisdom and perspective to a world that, as the COVID-19 pandemic proved, can never take anything for granted.

For that reason, I begin this book, like Chaucer's pilgrim on the road to Canterbury, telling a few well-worn stories in hopes of praising the past, warning for the present and charting a path for those who follow me in the future.

One of Chaucer's triumphs in *The Canterbury Tales* was putting the stories of his fourteenth-century characters into common English — not the French or Latin of "refined" society. So, if my vernacular sometimes sounds less like a banker and more like the Miller or the Cook, you can blame the great English poet. Many people thought Chaucer was writing for the court of his day, but the everyday tales, the bawdy stories of the common people preserved in *The Canterbury Tales*, belie that misconception. Likewise, some will look at the title of this book and think it is meant only for the financial crowd. But my purpose, like Chaucer's, is to write in the voice of all our customers, not a chosen few. So, enjoy.

CHAPTER 2

In the Eye of the Storm:
The Merger That Never Was

For Saint Paul says that all that's written well
Is written down some useful truth to tell.
Then take the wheat and let the chaff lie still.
— GEOFFREY CHAUCER, *The Canterbury Tales*

I think of the "post non-merger crisis" as probably my finest hour professionally at Bank of Montreal. What had begun in anticipation of a brave new Canadian banking world was suddenly "man the pumps" for us. The aftermath of our proposed merger with Royal Bank of Canada in 1998 was a survival-level strategy in many ways. We had put our credibility on the line, and when the deal didn't work out, we had to restore that credibility with our own employees. The challenges posed by not receiving government approval were numerous and daunting — and if not addressed properly, potentially quite damaging.

As many directors and colleagues at BMO will recall, the fallout from the "merger that never was" with RBC required us to face some unpleasant truths about ourselves. Maybe we had gone too far too fast? Maybe we needed to take a fresh look at our priorities?

When you think about the permutations and combinations of what could have gone wrong, we still managed to keep ourselves remarkably non-dysfunctional at a very difficult time. We were talking about the largest corporate merger ever in Canada. At 85,000 workers, the organization would have become the country's largest single non-governmental employer. It would have had $453 billion in assets and a stock-market valuation of $39 billion. Combined, it would have been the tenth-largest financial institution in North America and twenty-second in the world. It wouldn't be exaggerating to say that joining with RBC would have been the most significant merger in Canadian business history up to then. But it was not to be.

Like the best families, we rallied 'round one another and the organization when the proverbial chips were down. Managing BMO in the aftermath was, however, a classic example of managing the expectations we had created for ourselves when the merger was first announced.

People on Bay Street were talking about how they would always remember where they were when they first heard the news of the proposed merger between RBC and BMO, much as people talk about what they were doing when the Canadian hockey team beat the Soviet team in 1972. And in some ways it was just as emotional. Naturally, employees of both banks worried. *Will I still have a job? Customers fretted. Will you still be my Royal Bank or my Bank of Montreal? Are you going to go away?* Now, from the perspective of twenty-something years later, the high-stakes drama seems like ancient history. But it was all very real and very challenging — for our customers and our employees, and for us to manage through.

There was no dramatic moment at which the merger came to life; it was more gradual. I first became aware of the merger talk between us and the Royal Bank in the mid-1990s, when the whole process of consolidation was ramping up — which is, after all, a natural functioning of a market economy. The trust companies and brokerage houses were disappearing, so merger or buyout talk was not entirely unusual for the times. Matthew Barrett, BMO's CEO at the time, and I had seen it before with the Bank's acquisition of the Harris Bank of Chicago in 1984. That gave us full operating capability in the United States and a window into their market. Thus, the concept of consolidation and a merger with RBC was just a natural extension of the trend in financial service, and the evolution of the financial-service industry. We just had to convince the government of that thinking.

When I look in the rear-view mirror at the government's intervention, it's easy to see why they blocked the deal; they simply would not approve that much concentration in the sector. Our attempt to compete through size on the world stage was seen by them as an impediment to competition here at home. We had known that the proposed union would face some headwinds, but we also knew there had already been plenty of other mergers in the past. Look at the Imperial Bank of Canada merging with the Canadian Bank of Commerce in 1961 (the largest merger between chartered banks in Canadian history till then). And in 1955, you had the merger of Bank of Toronto and The Dominion Bank. So this was not necessarily new stuff. In fact, there seemed a kind of inevitability to it; there had been twenty-three banks in Canada in 1919, and by the late 1990s, there were only six.

When you get down to six banks, any fewer than that becomes more problematic in the public domain. There are concerns with concentration — we were not unaware of that. But the banks had decided they needed to grow so they could compete in the emerging global capital markets — it was that or get swallowed by foreign competitors themselves. And that's where, without a merger, the expectations of impending crisis came into it. Part of the way we had sold the merger in the media was: if this doesn't happen, it's a failure and we're destined to collapse. Not in so many words, but that was the underlying message. Dire, it goes without saying, in the financial world. And, what we hadn't fully anticipated in trying to sell ourselves to the government and the media that way was that we had created our own monster when the merger failed to happen: the public and our own employees were afraid that what we'd predicted would come to pass.

I still see absolutely nothing surprising in the federal government's response to our proposal. They had few options, given the social push-back on the potential for price increases and lack of competitiveness — which, by the way, was exactly the reaction in 1890 when there was an earlier wave of consolidation. In that year the furor was probably even worse than the outcry over our merger with the Royal Bank and for exactly for the same reasons. (The reason I know that is thanks to John Turley-Ewart's doctoral thesis, "Gentlemen Bankers, Politicians and Bureaucrats: The History of the Canadian Bankers Association, 1891–1924," which was more about the consolidation phase of the time rather than a history of the CBA.) It was just as bad then, maybe worse, as the big banks swallowed the little guys.

Now the official debate over our proposed merger in 1998 was whether we, Bank of Montreal and Royal Bank, had given proper involvement and notice to the government before we had embarked on our plan. In their decision, the Liberal government of the day didn't say these kinds of mergers should *never* happen. The rejection, they said, should not be seen as a "not now, not ever" prohibition of deals such as these. Rather, it should be understood and evaluated in the political context in which it was made. The merger proponents at Royal and Bank of Montreal wanted the deal to change the status quo, but the government of the day believed in the status quo as it existed in 1998.

Probably the biggest factor in the rejection, and this is all on the public record, was that Paul Martin, the finance minister at the time, actually had a keen instinct for the local politics of the issue. I never faulted him for that, because politicians have to respond to the concerns of the public they represent — in this case, the families of the people who might lose jobs. Notwithstanding that, we were hoping that the greater good from a market economy point of view would trump the enmity of the local sentiment. But Martin read that political pressure differently. In the long run, I was not surprised when it got turned down.

Apropos of nothing, as soon as we'd announced our plan to merge, CIBC and TD Bank decided suddenly they had better do a merger too. And so they submitted *their* merger proposal, kind of as a defensive action. I mean, if they thought the Royal Bank/BMO merger might get turned down, wouldn't theirs get rejected, too? And more to the point, if the government might allow one, they for sure wouldn't allow two. So it was a bit of a defensive play, in my opinion — unlikely to come off from either point of view, but a gambit they probably felt they had to lay down nonetheless.

The following year, when I was appointed CEO of Bank of Montreal in February 1999, all this noise and pressure — the fallout from the non-merger — was still very fresh. One of my biggest concerns was what the staff were thinking and feeling. *"Well, Tony, you've inherited this thing, what are you going to do to?" "What do we do next?" "Can we survive?"*

Emotions were running high, insecurity was rampant, and it was a huge challenge to manage the situation internally, as well as for our customers and shareholders. We had to focus on rejuvenating the goals and expectations of the Bank, and it took the next five years to do so.

At that challenging time, we were dealing with employee and public expectations and everyone asking, "How do we get back on track?" The answer is simple: by returning to basics and ignoring all the outside noise. My task was to get their focus off the recent past and onto how we could win the game going forward. Like, "Alright guys, that was then, this is now." Back to basics.

After the merger was rejected, I focused on how we were going to improve our game — that's when you really, really grind down. I brought in a couple of initiatives. For a long time, I thought that we hadn't really taken a look at how we allocated our capital on a line-of-business basis. And if you had looked at it, you would quickly come to the conclusion that there were about thirty-two discrete lines of business within BMO. I engaged Peter Kontes, who was running a company called Marakon, to do a lot of critical thinking about capital allocation in our business. We got really focused on taking a serious look at this stuff.

I said, "It's been a wonderful run and all, but with the merger gone that game is over. Our performance is still, at best, middle of the pack. So now, guys, this game is on. Back to basics." And we went into something called value-based management — which is when you make the interests of the shareholders paramount. This came as quite an eye-opener to all of us — especially to our corporate banking colleagues, whose client relationships were based on low-returning large loans and lines of credit. Accurate calculation of the capital to support these facilities had not been done in our bank, nor in other banks as far as I understood. We looked extremely closely at the allocation of capital, primarily in the corporate lending business, and dramatically changed it. And as a result, the return on capital started to go up.

The second thing I concentrated on was the area of productivity, or what the banks now call their operating leverage, which is the simple ratio of revenue to expenses. Back then we were not even in the middle of the pack among the banks; we were on the low end of the pack. Being research-oriented, I wanted to figure out before we started how I could create shareholder value and return on equity if I really focused on improving the operating leverage.

We began with a no-stone-left-unturned analysis of the current and future value-creating capacities of our many businesses. I solicited the help of a couple of my buddies whom I respected and we looked back across the industry over twenty-five and thirty years at the relative stock price performance related to the operating ratio. And why is that important? Because operating expenses relative to revenues were one of the few things we could control on our own. By focusing on those expenses we dramatically improved the ratio, gradually earning more return on capital, and the share price performance started to nudge its way up.

The world was not always kind to us as we pushed ahead with our transformation. The businesses we were exiting may have been under-performing, but they had been producing revenues that suddenly weren't there anymore. The media and investors wondered what we were doing. On the one hand, we had this downward pressure on earnings; on the other, it was too early to see any payoff from our strategically redeployed dollars. A tough spot.

Well, we did survive, but it took an enormous effort. Making some of the toughest decisions that boards and leadership teams ever get called on to make, we undertook the most radical restructuring in BMO's history. We became very clear on our purpose in life: the creation of shareholder value. Every decision we've taken since has been from that perspective. I would never in my maddest moments want to go through anything like that again, but I'll always be proud of being the guy at the helm through it all. As BMO responded and turned around, the bruising was more than worth it.

Ironically, the failure of the merger led to a kind of bank-to-bank consolidation anyway. The Big Six banks had a lot in common in terms of the business and our processes, and we didn't need a merger to find benefits and efficiencies in cooperating. Of course we were competitors, but it was more of a friendly competition rather than cutthroat. We knew that we were all basically in the same business and the guy who did a better job of looking after the clients might get some business one day, and the next day the other guy might get it.

Unlike Kraft and Unilever, for example, we weren't differentiated by intellectual property and couldn't really compete on that basis. We had more in common than we had differences, and we all shared the same business issues, such as, how can we improve the paper flow of the cheque process? How are you going to even compete in cheque processing? You're not, but by tackling those kinds of fundamental mechanical issues together the banks were taking into consideration efficiencies and economies of scale. In the aftermath of the non-merger, we were able to cooperate with our biggest competitors, uniting in areas where there wasn't really competition to create businesses — like Moneris (for credit card and debit payment processing) and Symcor, while focusing on the Canadian Depository for Securities (CDS), which benefitted all of us on the bottom line.

Not to be immodest but, based on our common needs in the industry, I helped invent Symcor Services, which is now one of the biggest payment-processing companies in the world. It was my mission to convince the other banks that we should get together on this, creating an outside company to serve us all. That didn't happen easily.

First I floated the idea to align our cheque-processing facilities, because it was ridiculous for all of us to have this kind of technology. "You can process cheques for all six of us with one machine. Why have six?" And they'd say, "Oh yeah, great idea, Tony," but it wouldn't actually happen. So then I thought, the only way to do this is to divide and conquer. I went to Royal Bank and said, "How about we do it together? We'll get significant scale, better than anything else." Once Royal Bank got on board and the other guys heard about this, it took nanoseconds for them to say, "Oh, we'd better get in on this or we'll get left behind."

Cooperation like that happens in the industry all the time. Even at the local level, the branch managers of Bank of Montreal and Royal Bank probably have lunch once a month or so. There is always some ongoing dialogue between colleagues from different banks; not necessarily about mergers or discussions of anything at that level, but about the business in general. And it happens on an international scale as well. For example, an American organization, now called the Bank Policy Institute (formed in 2018 by the merger of the Financial Services Roundtable and the Clearing House Association), would gather eighty to one hundred top CEOs of the banks in the U.S. twice a year, sometimes three times a year, and they would routinely invite the Canadian bank CEOs to be part of that. We all became very collegial, even in the midst of a period of consolidation in the banking industry in the United States. They were very productive meetings, because, as I say, there's a lot of commonality in regulatory oversight, technical infrastructure and so on, and sharing information on these issues was in the interest of all of us in the industry.

Consolidating and sharing resources have been happening in banking forever. It was very interesting when Visa came to town. The company was known as Chargex at the time. The Bank of America started it in 1958 in California and gradually it took hold, coming to Canada in 1968. The other banks — Scotia, Royal, Commerce and TD — all got into Chargex. At Bank of Montreal, we were so heavily embroiled in the building of the online banking system (more on that later) that we missed the initial entry into the charge-card market. When we finally did want in, Chargex said, "Well, Mr. Bank of Montreal, if you want to come in, the deal's going to be nine million bucks."

Gulp. That was an enormous investment back in the early '70s. (Adjusted for inflation, they were asking for a late-entry fee in the order of $55 million in today's dollars.) So we decided to pass on that, thank you very much. It soon became obvious that this credit-card processing thing was absolutely essential to the banking business, and we weren't part of it. We decided in 1972 that we had no choice — we *had* to do this. I was just up from programmer training school at this point, and I was immediately assigned to the Mastercard project. Because Chargex wouldn't allow us in we'd decided to go with Mastercard, their main competitor.

Visa and Mastercard were like that for a long time, and rigid adherence to competitive boundaries often translates into inefficiencies and duplication of resources. As I will describe in Chapter 22, Matt Barrett later broke the back of detrimental competitiveness when we combined our card-processing function with Royal Bank's. In December 2000 we created Moneris: a joint-venture company between the Bank of Montreal and the Royal Bank to handle card processing at the merchant level instead of doing it separately. Although the card business itself was competitive, we were still able to cooperate to reduce our investment in it and to increase bottom-line benefits.

Unfortunately, that cooperative spirit hadn't helped us when the merger failed in the late 1990s. After the non-merger, we had to bring focus back to our business and dig to find ways to improve it so we could remain competitive going forward. If you want to know what kind of people we are at BMO Financial Group, consider the effort that turned us around following the merger attempt and how collective it was, because it *had* to be. We converted that moment of truth into one of BMO's finest hours. As a result, our businesses are healthy, successful, and poised for further growth.

One of our senior directors said some wonderfully complimentary things that were passed on to me after I retired as CEO of the Bank. This is not intended to be self-aggrandizement, but I was very gratified when he said, "One of the things we've done wrong is we've failed to recognize the contribution that Tony made in the immediate collapse of the proposed merger."

Of course, the merger attempt and its aftermath don't begin to describe the challenges and satisfactions in my forty-plus years at Bank of Montreal. So perhaps I should start at the beginning.

TONY'S TAKEAWAY

The legendary boxer Mike Tyson said everyone has a plan till they get punched in the mouth. I know, he's not exactly a business philosopher but he has a point. Preparing for and dealing with the worst means being flexible and adaptable and having a long-term vision for where you're going.

VOICE: **BILL DOWNE** CM

Bill Downe and I have been colleagues at Bank of Montreal for a long time. Our immediate collaboration in running the Bank came about only when I made Bill head of invest-ment banking. Talk about an inspired appointment! Bill did a first-class job running our investment bank, then an inspired job guiding the Bank through the 2008 financial crisis. Bill has wonderful and shared values, supporting numerous charitable and public service institutions in both Canada and the United States. I admire him greatly and consider him a valued friend.

From the time I joined Bank of Montreal in 1983, what was instilled in me — flowing from Tony's influence through progressive levels of the organization — was that as managers we had an obligation to our shareholders, our customers, our employees and the communities we served. This idea was decades advanced from the focus on the environ-ment, governance and society that is being so widely discussed today. I was acutely aware of this as a touchstone of our business model. Tony was a carrier of this disciplined framework that defined what we owe to shareholders in proper context; economic value added was the conse-quence of the intentional balancing of the four dimensions of the scorecard. Happily, the Bank has continued this tradition.

I have great respect for Tony and appreciation for the opportunities he gave me when he was in a top leadership position. He is an introspec-tive person, and I had limited glimpses of him when I worked for him in the early years. In fact, it wasn't until after I was appointed vice-chair of Bank of Montreal in the late '90s — when he invited me to play golf with him in a charity pro-am tournament — that I spent any one-on-one time with him. His communication style can be quite formal, and it was unusual for me at the time.

I learned a great deal from my association with Tony and benefitted from his sponsorship. He introduced me to the board at St. Michael's Hospital after we had talked about how I might be more involved in the Toronto community, given that I had spent much of my career in other cities. It personified his influence on me; he played an important part in my development and understanding of the role of the Bank in the broader community. BMO now has an employee giving program in which over 90 percent of employees participate, the origins of which reside in Tony's early work. As well, his legacy of championing diversity and inclusion within the Bank continues today, with no less than 40 percent of senior roles filled by women.

Tony is a man of enormous integrity and fairness, and my time with him was highly productive. I have warm affection for him.

CHAPTER 3

First Contact: BMO in the Blood

He who repeats a tale after a man,
Is bound to say, as nearly as he can,
Each single word, if he remembers it,
However rudely spoken or unfit,
Or else the tale he tells will be untrue,
The things invented and the phrases new.
— GEOFFREY CHAUCER, *The Canterbury Tales*

Although this work is meant more as a meditation on my forty-year career at BMO rather than a conventional autobiography, a little background about my early years and how I came to work at the Bank of Montreal might be in order. My grandfather, Harry Christian Comper, was born an Anglican in England. The family has a long tradition of Harry then Henry then Harry then Henry for the first-born male — we have traced our family tree back to the mid-sixteenth century in France. The detail about his religious affiliation is significant because family apocrypha suggests that his ancestors likely were originally Protestants in France. Persecuted along with the rest of the Huguenots, they fled France for England after the revocation of the Edict of Nantes in 1598 and went to Sussex in southern England.

According to family lore they were pewterers. I have a pewter tea service that was a wedding gift from my parents as a tribute to the family's roots as metalsmiths. My distant cousin was Sir John Ninian Comper (1864–1960), a church architect of some prominence in Britain in the early part of the twentieth century, noted for re-introducing the idea of the "English altar," an altar surrounded by riddel posts. Sir John Betjeman who, as you may or may not know, was Poet Laureate of the United Kingdom from 1972–84, was a great lover of the other Sir John's Gothic Revival work.

My Comper cousin was a Scottish-born Anglican church architect who believed in designing churches in their entirety, including not only the architecture of the building itself, but also the rood screen and the furnishings. He worked with a group of Anglican nuns who, after he'd designed the garments, would make them for use in the church. Reportedly they were very attractive and he became quite famous for them. He also did the stained-glass windows of the north wall of the nave in Westminster Abbey, which unfortunately were blown up by bombs in World War II. In fact, Sir John's remains are buried in Westminster Abbey. Betjeman did the eulogy at his funeral in 1960.

The last time I was in London, I went to visit the restored windows, which are Sir John Comper's tribute to the great philanthropists. The guide pointed me to one image in particular and I went to look closer. And, what do you know, it was one of my predecessors at Bank of Montreal, Lord Strathcona, who was president of the Bank in the late nineteenth century and, with his first cousin Lord Mount Stephen — who had also, incidentally, been a Bank of Montreal president — co-founded the Canadian Pacific Railway. Lord Strathcona later became famous for driving the Last Spike to commemorate the completion of the huge engineering feat that was the CPR in 1885.

Back to my immediate clan. My sister Betty (she's three years older than me and lives in Chippewa, Ontario, with her husband, a former high school teacher) and I have different theories about what motivated my grandfather to leave England and emigrate to Canada. For whatever reason he arrived on these shores in 1914, Grandfather came to Toronto with between four and six children. He wound up living in a house on Oak Street in Cabbagetown. They were very poor, because Grandfather wasn't working regularly. I was told that the house — again, this may be a bit of apocrypha — had a dirt floor and a privy in the backyard, not indoor plumbing. In any event, Toronto was not the same modern, cosmopolitan place it is today. The first winter they were here in Canada, it was going to be a pretty bleak Christmas for my grandfather and grandmother and their young kids, including my father.

The story goes that Grandmother's brother back in England was fairly well-to-do. He had some shares in Canadian Pacific, and so he mailed his poor sister a CP dividend cheque drawn on the Bank of Montreal. (This was long after the Bank of Montreal had financed the Canadian Pacific Railway.) The cheque arrived on or around their first Christmas Eve in Canada and the five-pound dividend in British sterling was considered a lot of money in those days. (You'd need about £380 in today's money to match the buying power.)

Grandmother walked from Cabbagetown to the Queen and Yonge branch of Bank to Montreal and went in to see if she could convert this precious cheque. Somehow she ended up talking directly to the branch manager about cashing the dividend. There was nothing wrong with the cheque — it was *bona fide*. The manager looked at her and said, "Mrs. Comper, I'll cash this cheque for you on one condition: that you only ever deal with the Bank of Montreal." She was so pleased to be talking to the manager that she agreed to his terms. He dutifully cashed the cheque for her. She got twenty-five or thirty dollars Canadian, which was a lot of money in those days. She went straight over to Eaton's and bought a turkey and other food and presents for the kids. It turned out to be a wonderful first Christmas in Canada for the family, courtesy of Grandmother's brother, the CPR and the Bank of Montreal.

Grandmother dealt only with the Bank of Montreal from then on, just as she had promised, and she instructed the rest of the family to use the Bank of Montreal exclusively as well. She was a loyal customer, and it became the family banking connection. Not surprisingly, my dad Frank Comper always had a fondness for Bank of Montreal growing up. That sort of bond was not that unusual in those days, and that's why I tell employees today that personal connections can be an important building block for the Bank.

My mother's family, the Dubés, were French Canadians from Rivière-du-Loup. Her father, Hippolyte Nil Dubé, was a haberdasher. When that business failed, he later emigrated to Marengo, Saskatchewan, in the early twentieth century to homestead. It was a tough life, and many walked away from the homesteads that were offered by the government. (You had to last three years and only then would they give you the deed.) But Mom, who had the elegant name of Marie-Noelle Marie-Antoinette Dubé, and her family, stuck it out. (There's also a wonderful railway connection to Bank of Montreal on the Prairies that I'll get into in Chapter 21.) She came east after the war to train as a nurse, and that's when she met my father.

In the years leading up to the Great Depression, my dad was still just a kid and, like the rest of his siblings, he had to work to help support the family — Grandfather was an intellectual and, to my estimation, seemingly wasn't too enthusiastic about getting employment himself. (Grandfather did, however, make the acquaintance of Stephen Leacock when the family was holidaying up near Lake Simcoe and they corresponded for a time.) When he was just a young man, my father wound up getting a job with Commercial Credit in 1920. He had just gotten his junior matriculation from De La Salle College, which is where I later went to school myself. He, his sisters and his brother Bill all wound up in the financial industry and they, in turn, financed the family.

Dad had a long career with Commercial Credit Corporation, who were in the sales-finance business. These types of companies don't exist anymore, but they were quite common when I was growing up. They made their money because the banks were constrained in terms of the rate of interest that they could charge their retail clients. The retail automobile business was built on automobile dealers who were financing the cars they were selling to their customers through dealer floor plans. The sales-finance companies — Commercial Credit Corporation and a few others — would borrow wholesale from the bank and then lend to the dealers at higher rates of interest to fund their floor plans. Companies like Commercial Credit were arbitraging, a middle-man kind of thing. It was all above-board and there were regulations on what they were doing. It was a big business for a long while. (However, it began to disappear as a consequence of the 1964 Porter Banking Commission, which mandated the abolition of the 6 percent interest-rate ceiling on bank loans, disclosure of bank-loan costs, entry of banks into conventional mortgage financing and legislation to prevent banks from agreeing to set common interest rates, chequing costs and other customer charges.)

When I turned sixteen, my dad decided that I was having too much fun and I should have a summer job myself. Through his commercial contacts, he approached two bankers, one at Royal Bank and the other at Bank of Montreal. He approached the Royal Bank manager first and said, "Do you have a summer job for my kid?"

They didn't.

So he went to Bank of Montreal. He approached Dick Jones, the first-assistant manager of the King and Yonge branch in Toronto, who also happened to live down the street from us in Leaside. You've got to understand that that branch had 100 people on staff at the time — huge by today's standards. It was the go-to branch in those days, one of the principal bankers to the whole investment bank and securities community. So Dick Jones, top assistant branch manager of three assistant branch managers lobbied strenuously with the forces of darkness at Bank of Montreal's human resources department, and I wound up getting a summer job as a messenger. Because of the size of the King and Yonge branch, we had six messengers doing all the routine commercial procedures and exchanges of the Bank, which was a big deal. That was my summer job all the way through high school and then during university. I majored in English Literature at the University of St. Michael's College at the University of Toronto, but every summer I'd go back to the Bank, working there on a seasonal basis from 1961 until 1967 — when I was faced with deciding which professional route I was going to take.

I talk a lot about intangible assets in business and in life, and if there's one theme that I hope runs through this book, it is the importance of relationships. Relationships are an intangible asset. They were important to my grandmother, the first link in a long-lasting family connection to the Bank of Montreal. They were important in how my dad got me started at the Bank. And they are very important in our business today. In fact, most of the business that we do in banking is based on relationships. We're not selling hard goods or natural resources, and what we sell is not that much different from the products and services of other financial institutions. Our unique selling proposition is based on the people in our business — staff and customers. Even when I was doing corporate lending, it was based on relationships and based on trust.

I can trace my long career at the Bank back to that random and somewhat coincidental first encounter of my grandmother's, and certainly to the professional connections my father had established in the financial industry. Funny sidebar about my dad: years after I'd started as a messenger and many promotions later, Bank of Montreal sent me to London, England, in 1984 to run the branch there. Dad, of course, was very proud of the progress I was making in the Bank, even if he didn't always have a clear idea of what exactly I was doing as I gained experience and moved up the ranks.

So, when I called him up with the exciting news of this latest promotion, I said, "Dad, you know what, I'm moving to London. They're going to make me manager of our London branch." He said, "Jesus, Tony, I knew if you hung in there long enough you'd get to be a branch manager." True story. I'd already been a vice-president and in charge of large departments at the Bank. In fact, I'd been the youngest vice-president ever. It was the funniest thing. He didn't understand all the subtleties and the inside baseball of being a senior vice-president, but he understood the prestige of being a branch manager from his days in the business. And I had gotten to be a branch manager: that was his definition of success.

TONY'S TAKEAWAY

Creating loyalty is a full-time job. It's never too early to convince customers that they are safe in your care. In my many years at the Bank, I never stopped impressing on our staff that developing customer loyalty is a full-time job. And that goes for any business: it's never too early to convince customers that they are safe in your care.

VOICE: MIRANDA HUBBS

Miranda Hubbs was my colleague on the board of Spectra Energy, a Houston-based U.S. energy company. She was a highly successful investment banker and is now a corporate director who also devotes time as a senior director of the Canadian Red Cross. She is a major funder and supporter of contemporary art initiatives — notably the Toronto Biennial.

I first met Tony at his office in First Canadian Place where he was set to interview me for a role on the Spectra Energy board of directors. I am sure he is aware of how intimidating it can be to enter the hallowed halls of the executive floor of the Bank to meet with the former CEO of BMO. He was kind, charming and disarming and his demeanour put me at ease.

After that meeting, Tony endorsed and championed me, and I was invited to join the Spectra board — my first board role. On our flights to and from board meetings in Houston, our conversations soon stretched beyond business and ran the gamut from art and literature to philosophy and religion, to history and blockchain technology. His knowledge is as extensive as his interests are varied, and I looked forward to the wisdom he imparted.

This is what I knew of Tony, the man. Then one day during a particularly animated board meeting, the participants were getting a bit rambunctious and off-topic. Tony didn't say a word, but merely cleared his throat in a subtle signal of disapproval and, in an instant, the meeting was back on track and the room full of former Fortune 500 CEOs was back in line. He has a presence and leadership quality that commands the utmost respect. That was my first introduction to Tony, the CEO. I am honoured to call both Tonys mentor and friend.

CHAPTER 4

Choosing the Road Less Travelled

No empty-handed man can lure a bird.
— GEOFFREY CHAUCER, *The Canterbury Tales*

What was it that made a young fellow reading Chaucer, a University of Toronto guy, try banking as a career? Why would anyone in the Swinging Sixties want to go into banking when there were so many exciting jobs out there? It's a question I hear a lot from young people who think that every choice must tick off a box on a checklist for success.

I put it down to one thing: serendipity. I was following my dream, not even realizing that's what I was doing at the time. I went to De La Salle College in Toronto, a private Catholic school that offered a combination of very strong academics and very strong sports. In fact, former quarterback of the Toronto Argonauts and CFL Hall of Famer Nobby Wirkowski was the coach of our senior football team when I was there. The school was also very enlightened, I thought. The Christian Brothers who ran De La Salle believed that the academic program in most high schools in Ontario was too tame and too easy, so those of us in the scholarship class, myself included, shouldn't be allowed to wait until Grade 13, which we still had in those days, to write all our higher exams in preparation for university.

We were all on scholarship in that class: twenty partials and ten full (I was a partial), and we all had to write four Ontario Grade 13 exams in Grade 12, and nine more in Grade 13, so that we would have a total of thirteen credits — far more than the six the province required for graduation — and be eligible to pursue any course of study in any university. No matter what the high-school prerequisites were for your chosen specialty in university, you had them all after taking such a wide range of courses at Del and writing so many exams.

I thought that was pretty enlightened, actually, designing the curriculum so students would have unlimited choice for their postsecondary studies. But the Brothers also believed we should try to figure out what we were going to be when we grew up. So, in Grade 10, I had a great vocational guidance counsellor who ran me through several tests. One particular assessment, the Kuder Vocational Preference Test (I still have a copy of it; I'm a pack rat, by the way), wasn't to measure aptitude and it wasn't an IQ test; it was designed to determine what you liked, not what you were good at. I scored high in three areas: literary, computational — which was mathematics — and scientific. And I got virtually zero on everything else.

So I had a firm idea of the directions I shouldn't follow. But I had no focused idea of what I actually wanted to do yet — I had even thought of going into the priesthood at one time. I had started working summers at the Bank, but I didn't see one clear path forward, no calling I felt I must pursue. I decided to see if the muse would strike me by going to university. Fortunately, Commercial Credit Corporation, where my father worked, was a generous American company and they awarded me a scholarship to attend U of T. Thank God, otherwise I couldn't have afforded to go. There wasn't a lot of financial support available from Canadian universities back then, but off I went thanks to CCC's private scholarship.

When I finished my undergraduate degree, I thought I wanted to be an English professor, so I stayed on to pursue graduate studies in English at U of T. After the first year of graduate school, my marks weren't quite good enough to continue with a master's degree. U of T was pretty tough academically, particularly in the English department, and I admit, I had also fooled around a lot in my graduate year and enjoyed myself immensely. I played bass guitar in a band I'd cleverly called The Compleat Works in tribute to my literary studies — but I probably spent more time on the band than on those literary studies. Now, I thought, what's next?

I had worked at the Bank of Montreal for six summers by that point, and I thought maybe there could be something there for me in the short term. My timing was perfect: in 1967, for the first time in its history, the Bank of Montreal had decided to systematically recruit university graduates at an entry level. They called it the special development program, and it was structured to make you a branch manager in five years. I thought, I'll join the bank and go from there. I could get a job, make some money and do something real. And after a year or so I figured I'd go to law school or into the investment banking side of the business or something. I know it probably sounds a little imprecise, but remember: it was the '60s.

And so the Bank accepted me into their special development program but added, "Now, Tony, it's already July; we started the program in June, and you're a month behind all the other guys. We don't know whether you'll be able to keep up or not after losing a month of learning. But we'll try you."

It took me about three seconds to complete all the courses. I'm not bragging, it's just I had been working at a very big branch. I'd worked in every single department and knew all the routines for foreign exchange, securities and lending. The other kids in the program had no idea how any of that worked yet, so I looked like a genius by comparison.

With those results, I was now on track to become a branch manager in five years. They started moving me around to gain even more varied experience. In those days, before computers were standard, you had to have skills for an industry that wasn't yet automated, at least not to the degree we know it today. All these different postings were where you learned the rudiments of everyday banking procedures and processes — all of which were manual and handed down from one generation of bankers to the next, rather than most of the routine procedures and transactions being taken care of by computers.

My first branch was in what they now call the Manulife Centre, but it was known simply as the Bay and Bloor branch at the time. It was easy work, because I had worked there before. Pat McCrimmon, who was in the special development program as well, was at the Bay and Bloor branch with me. The other thirteen were at different branches, but we were getting to know each other a little.

Every month we'd go downtown for another phase of learning and exams. It was boring for me but all part of the program. My next branch was Leaside, and that was where I became an accountant in training. In those days we didn't have what are now called assistant branch managers — we called them accountants, which was the British term for that job. It was a very handy location, because I could walk out the back door of our home into the lane behind the Leaside stores and walk up to the branch. After six months of training, they transferred me to Roselawn and Yonge, my first appointment as a full-fledged accountant; that was a big deal. I was moving up the ladder.

The powers that be decided to test me in a couple of bailout jobs. This would become characteristic of the rest of my story at the Bank until the day I left. I was a stabilizer, the turnaround guy. They wanted to move me downtown to start the credit-officer phase of the training program, but my district manager said, "No, no. I've got a couple of real problems I need Tony to fix. The Eglinton and Hilltop branch has got a big problem. The branch manager's not well, and I need a caretaker manager for a period of time to at least stabilize the place." I said, "Yeah, but I haven't done any of that." He said, "Don't worry about that. You go in there, and you'll stabilize the place. We know we can trust you." So I did, for a short period of time.

Finally, after a lot of pressure from King and Yonge I wound up back downtown again. But now I was a credit officer grade two. That was a terrific experience, going back to my home branch but now in a much different capacity. That's where I learned all about lending. That was 1969, and I was only two years into a five-year program. That's how they worked in those days: there was no time to let the dust settle.

Then one fine day, I received a phone call out of the blue from somebody at head office in Montreal. "Tony, I'm going to take you out to lunch." *What's this about? What trouble spot do they want me in now?* I thought.

Gard Robertson, the person on the phone, wasn't a banking type. He had come over to head office from Ford Motor Company to help them beef up human resources because the focal point of upgrading the workforce at the Bank was going to be HR-driven from the head office. (The head office of Bank of Montreal was still in Montreal in those days, but that's a story for another chapter.) The Bank had hired McKinsey & Company in 1966 to figure out why we weren't making more progress. They were there as consultants to explain everything about vertical integration, branch presence, market share and so on. One of McKinsey's recommendations was that the Bank needed to get serious about its human-resources practices, and Gard was part of that movement. (True story: I was told that a senior executive in 1968 asked a personnel department executive for a copy of the departmental budget, and the executive replied, "Budget? No one has ever asked us to prepare one." That story is unthinkable today.)

So, Gard took me out to lunch. "Tony, we have this fantastic opportunity," he said. "We've got some great jobs on offer in Montreal at head office. We would like you to come down and think about a job we're calling Recruitment Coordinator. You would help us recruit young university graduates."

That was for the very same special development program I was still in, and now they wanted me to seek out and hire other people like me? So I asked, "Why would I be interested in this? I'm on track to become a branch manager in five years."

He said, "Well, as a branch manager, your sales potential is basically a zero in the marketplace. But if you get a fancy job in something like human resources in Montreal, it's a much better credential on your résumé." He had my attention. Then he said, "By the way, you're on a management grade two?"

"Yeah."

Then he *really* got my attention when he said, "The job we've got in mind for you is a management grade seven."

Wow, that was an unprecedented jump. And more money. That sounded alright to me, so I said, "Okay, what happens next?"

"I go back and talk to them about doing an interview if you're interested."

"Well, I want to learn more about it."

"You might have to come down to Montreal for an interview."

I thought, okay, I can do that. My boss at this time was a very intelligent woman by the name of Joyce Acton. I said to Joyce, "I had this job offer." And she said, "Nobody around here knows about it, Tony, so shut up." I took her excellent advice and shut up.

After that, I didn't hear anything for about six weeks and I thought maybe the job offer had gone away. I figured I was still doing my credit officer thing en route to a bank manager's job, and I was fine with that. So I sort of forgot all about it.

They did eventually decide at head office that they wanted to wheel me down to Montreal for a formal interview there. But they had to clear it with the HR department and the branch people. That's how the higher-ups at the King and Yonge branch found out that head office had done an end-run around them, talking to me and offering me this job in Montreal. And they were annoyed.

I found myself being taken out to lunch again, this time at the Albany Club by Dick Jones, the man who'd hired me six years earlier as a summer hire. "Tony, they've offered you this job," he said. "I was kind of upset, because I hired you here and you're on this program and the Bank's been good to you. Now, they're doing an end-run around me, offering you this big job." He continued, "One thing you're going to learn is that when you're in staff jobs in head office, they've always got job grades that are inflated. Why? Because they control the grading process." He was right, of course. Then he said, "If you want to do that, then Godspeed; you go with my blessing. But everybody else in divisional headquarters is really annoyed. So you'd better be careful. Just be nice to people." It was good advice.

Soon I heard from head office: "Tony, you've got to come to Montreal for an interview with all the brass." On November 11, 1970, I flew to Montreal. It was the first time I'd ever been on an airplane. They met me at the Airport Hilton in Dorval, where I did the interview and flew straight back the same day. At this point, I was seriously dating Liz, and she and my kid brother met me at the Toronto airport. They wanted to know how the interview went, but I was more excited about it being my first airplane trip. All I wanted to talk about was the plane ride — I didn't give a darn about the job interview.

Once again, I didn't hear anything until about four weeks later, close to Christmas, when I got a message saying, "You've got the job. And you're to come to Montreal again. We want you to come down just to talk to a few people to get oriented." I went in the second week of December, and that's when I met Matt Barrett, the guy who was going be my colleague for the next few decades, all the way to the C-suite at BMO. I also met Harriet Stairs, a woman who was going be another one of my colleagues — and who would ultimately become head of human resources at the Bank. And I finally met Bob MacDougall, the manager of the new computer department for which I would be recruiting. Bob would eventually become my boss. I was to report for my first day of work on the first business day of January.

New year, new job, new city. A whole new world.

I flew to Montreal after New Year's and stayed in the Holiday Inn on Sherbrooke Street for the first month. It was the winter of 1969–70, and my most vivid memory of my first day at head office was walking down St. James Street to get there — it was so damned cold I actually got frostbite on one ear. In fact, I think it didn't get above 0° Fahrenheit (that's -17° Celsius) in Montreal for the whole month of January that year. I thought, "What have I gotten myself into?"

Looking back, I think it was just kind of blind luck that I ended up in Montreal. They had an inventory of fifteen university graduates, and it was was the first time that they had formally recruited a cohort of trainees with these credentials. Sure, there had been some other accidental hires like that in the past, but this was a formal program. In looking to beef up the newly minted HR department, which was going to be the engine for retooling the manpower of the Bank and building it for the future, they probably looked at us and thought, "We've got all these bright young university kids who are in this pilot program. Let's see if we can pick off a few of those." I was kind of the trial balloon.

So I arrived at BMO Head Office in Montreal, and I was suddenly a "Recruitment Coordinator" along with Matt Barrett. His job was recruiting for head office, including the secretarial staff. My job was to help build the incipient computer department, a function that was only beginning to emerge in the business world: I was to recruit young kids to become computer types.

At this point, I knew almost nothing about computers. Before moving to Montreal I had started taking an MBA at nights at U of T. One of the courses, which I found really interesting, was an introduction to programming in FORTRAN, a language for high-performance computing that IBM had developed in the '50s. So I had a rudimentary orientation in FORTRAN. But that was it.

At any rate, I went to Montreal and began hiring young people to staff the brand-new computer department, which was headed up by Bob MacDougall. Like Gard Robertson, Bob had been hired from Ford Motor Company, where he had installed a new human resources department and payroll system and had done it all under budget and in blinding speed. He was a genius. He was also a unique person; we had heard he had taken a year off to sail around the Caribbean with his family on a catamaran. I came to be terribly fond of him. He used to publish different classes of memos — some on pink paper, some on green paper, some on blue paper — depending on the audience for the thing. Many of them were written in cursive by hand, not on a typewriter, and he would write a multipage memo in one shot, with no editing, and it was totally understandable. A genius.

Sequestered with Bob to work on capital projections for the online banking system (I'll get to that in another chapter), I was now doing some really fascinating work. The Bank had invested millions of dollars to build this computer department, and they wanted it done fast. It was truly groundbreaking. To feed the machine, I was hiring young people as quickly as I could to fill positions for computer programmers and analysts. We didn't have the luxury of trying to maintain the status quo that was still alive in the banking industry — there was no boys' club here. The Bank hired anybody — it didn't matter if you were male or female. The hiring frenzy was quite intense and the whole business of computers was so new — it all felt a bit like the Wild West and we were the pioneers. But I was very attracted to the idea of this department and the work they were doing. I knew it was going to be significant — just *how* significant and challenging it would be was still to be revealed.

One of the guys there would eventually become my mentor when I took the leap into the world of computers myself, a chap by the name of Neville Shevloff, whom Bob MacDougall had hired from Canadair. Neville had been an engineer and technician at Short Brothers, the aircraft builders in Belfast, where they were installing very early computers, like Mercury delay lines, in the engineering department. He'd been given the assignment to be the go-to guy for HR to hire all these people, and he befriended me. So did his family. I was a young single guy in Montreal, and he and his wife had five kids — they kind of took me under their wing. I would be at their house for dinner three nights a week, and I went to their son's bar mitzvah.

Not long after I started hiring all these computer hotshots, I went to Neville and said, "You know what? I really like this environment, and it's clear to me that if I'm going to stick around this business, I've got to become a computer technician." And I boldly asked, "Do you think I could apply to come into the department and work here?"

"We'd love to have you," replied Neville.

I floated the idea by one of my bosses in HR, and he said, "Tony, you're nuts. These guys are a bunch of techies. You have a brilliant career ahead. I need you to finish this assignment in my department. Why would you want to go and put your whole career into something like this? We have no idea where the hell all this computer stuff is going."

"Sorry, I want to do this." With the self-assurance of youth, I did it anyway. And who could have known just how big all that "computer stuff" would become?

At that point, the Bank had just started a new version of a program they had been running, hiring people who had the aptitude to train as a computer programmer. To prove you had the aptitude, you had to take a test — I believe it was called the Wolf Test in Logical Reasoning Ability. Not only did you have to take it, you had to get at least 90 percent on it. I took it, got the marks and got accepted into the programmer training school — after a six-month stint, I was a newly minted application programmer.

The job grades for that new role were not that great, however. In fact, I had to take a four job–grade cut, from a management grade seven to a grade three. My former boss just said, "See?" But that wouldn't stop me. If I'd paused to think that I was throwing away my chance to be a branch manager — how I had previously defined a successful career path at the Bank — I might not have been so assured. But I had made up my mind.

TONY'S TAKEAWAY

A fulfilling career arc means being willing to leave the chosen road at times. Be open to new ways to reach your destination.

VOICE: JACK O'BRIEN, PART 1

Jack O'Brien and I met when he and I were 18, having just entered the seminary together, and at the same time, first-year students at the University of Toronto. In second year at university, fresh out of the seminary, we started a rock band, The Compleat Works. We've been friends since those days. Without me, the band plays on!

Tony and I met when we both began our first year of university as English majors at the University of St. Michael's College at the University of Toronto in September 1963. What put us in proximity of each other was our decision to enter St. Augustine's Seminary, which at the time had a "branch" on U of T's St. Michael's campus in a residence called Cloverhill. Of the roughly two dozen young men who entered that year, nine were first-year students, Tony and I among them.

Music, specifically the guitar, was our secondary point of connection. It turned out that one of the third-year seminarians played guitar — a Martin guitar at that — so every evening during recreation, which ran from 6:45 to 7:30 p.m., a virtual hootenanny occurred in the Cloverhill rec room where those of us who fancied learning to play were encouraged to strum along. Add to that the fact that Tony and I attended a number of the same classes, and that he and I often paired up on our habitual evening walk, and you can see that friendship was almost inevitable.

The cementing of said friendship began in earnest when Tony invited me to his house in Leaside either for Thanksgiving or the 1963 Grey Cup. (You'd think I would remember more clearly given that I didn't drink alcohol at the time, but fifty-plus years have dulled my memory. I lean towards the Grey Cup because I seem to remember lying on the carpet in his living room watching TV, but who knows.) Either way, that's when I met Tony's older sister Betty with her boyfriend Garth (or maybe fiancé by then), and his brothers Michael (a few years younger than Tony) and Paul (significantly younger than Michael). You only had to listen to Tony's mom pronounce in her stentorian voice who was going to do what and exactly when to figure out how appropriate her title The Enforcer was. She was a strong Catholic, and, though it didn't occur to me at the time, probably the driving force behind Tony's entering the seminary.

I never did find out why Tony quit the seminary (or if I did, I've forgotten). However, I learned much later that from day one Tony felt out-of-step with seminary life and many times had asked the rector for permission to go off on his own while the rest of us were confined to our rooms. So a one-year-and-out stay was pretty much inevitable for him. For my part, I hadn't given leaving any thought at all until I got a telephone call in the second week of July telling me that part of my responsibility as a seminarian was to act as a counsellor at a residential camp the following week. However, I had previously agreed to sing at a friend's wedding in the third week of July, and I was not about to miss that gig. Before I knew it, I had blurted out that I was pretty sure I didn't have a vocation and that I was quitting and wouldn't be at camp next week.

CHAPTER 5

The Catastrophizer

As you know, no master of a household
Has all of his utensils made of gold;
Some are wood, and yet they are of use.
— GEOFFREY CHAUCER, *The Canterbury Tales*

The best way to describe my personality is that I'm a catastrophizer. I always think that something's going to go wrong. But I also love problem-solving: if it's going to go wrong, then what's the backup plan, and how are we going to execute it? Catastrophizing has always come naturally to me. I was never surprised by things that blew up because I had always believed that they could and was always prepared when they did. And it was a funny feeling when things actually broke down, as if I was happy to test my solutions. As I think back now, even from the beginning of my career I would get parachuted into situations that were screwed up because the Bank knew I was a good catastrophizer and a problem-solver.

This personality trait was an asset in the huge software projects we were undertaking in the 1970s when I joined the computer department full-time as a programmer. I enjoyed the software culture, which is all about solving problems, and I believe I became even better at creating solutions as a result of my move into the computer department.

One of my first assignments as part of that group was the launch of the Mastercard program, which we were getting into belatedly. As mentioned earlier, we had decided to go with Mastercard instead of Chargex/Visa when it was necessary for banks to have credit card programs. We were the only major bank in Canada to go with Mastercard (originally known as Interbank from 1966 to 1969 and then Master Charge from 1969 to 1979).

To launch the Mastercard program, we bought a software package from Credit Systems Incorporated of St. Louis, Missouri, and I became a member of the project team tasked with installing it at BMO — we were going to Canadianize it and install it in Montreal. The Americans were much further along in terms of the application than us: they had an up-and-running software package and it was very detailed. Like a good catastrophizer, I looked at all the ways ours could fail, just to reassure myself. But it proved to be a big success.

The next program I was on was even bigger and more historic. It was the beginning of any-branch banking and, eventually, the ABM network. In those early days of computing and applying computing to business applications, the big issue — and it was an enormous under- taking — was building the beginnings of the online banking system we know today to allow instant communication branch-to-branch. It was revolutionary!

First, a little background. All of the computer applications that existed in the banks at that time went by the acronym of COLT: Canadian OnLine Teller. The main software application was resident in IBM's data centre in Toronto, and computer terminals in all the branches were connected to this application running at IBM. It would do transaction processing, debits and credits, update your passbook and that kind of stuff, all of which had been done manually up until then.

Still, BMO's idea was that there had to be something even more comprehensive than this. We were going to develop — the terminology seems so mundane now — a real-time system. With the IBM system the other banks were using, when you cashed your cheque and that transaction was posted, your account really wouldn't get updated until that night when IBM did what they called their offline processing. This process consisted of running all the files and gathering all the data that had been collected through the terminals in the banks' branches during the day and updating the master files. In the morning the customer would have an updated file.

This all happened on a regional level, not national. Our task was to eliminate the daily double processing of branch transactions on a branch terminal, and again overnight at IBM; to eliminate manual processing of transactions across regions; and to keep only one database for customer accounts, not an online database supporting branch terminals and a real database for customer accounts on computer tapes. Our boss said, "We're going to have a real-time system. You do the transaction on the terminal, it updates the database, that's it. Forever. There's no overnight processing. You have a real-time online banking system where your account is instantaneously updated universally across the country. So whether you're in Vancouver, whether you're in Toronto, one database."

Now, real-time nationwide was probably the most ambitious thing that had ever been invented in commercial software for financial institutions, or it certainly seemed like it. This software was cutting edge. Our programmers and technicians were creating programs that are now established commercial software that we take for granted, but what we now know as online banking wasn't even in the beta stage at that time. Hell, we were *inventing* it in concert with IBM. (Subsequently, this software was turned into a commercial product by IBM and became the standard for the financial industry. But it was developed by the people at Bank of Montreal with the IBM lab in Toronto.)

I am the still proud possessor of a punch-card deck — it's in my office to this day — of something called the TDMM, the Time Division Multiplexer Microprogram, which is the software that we wrote especially for the Bank to supplant the regional computers and communicate information on a national basis. It seems like child's play now, but it was thought to be very progressive at the time.

It would take several hours and many pages to tell you the entire drama of trying to get this thing working, because it didn't work at first. (No wonder I'm a catastrophizer!) To test it, we decided to put it into pilot locations, initially in just two branches in Ontario: Clinton and Exeter. The poor branches were struggling through being guinea pigs for this new thing we were creating. Then we got twenty-five more pilot branches online, and it was the same thing: it was bug-ridden and wouldn't work the way we had planned. The system was frequently down and pretty much felt like a catastrophe.

In the meantime, we also had much turnover in the technical department — there was just a small core group of about six to eight of us running the place, and I was a fairly junior guy with a management grade of ten or eleven or something at this point. (The top management grade was twenty-five or twenty-six at the time.) The department had lost a lot of the executives who were running it, for a whole series of reasons I won't get into. So this handful of us basically had to do everything to try to put this new system back on the air and get it up and running.

It was a huge financial commitment, and for the Bank there was no going back. Senior management really had no idea what we were doing. They didn't understand the software, so they couldn't be critical. I remember a discussion I had with one of our top executives at the time. He said, "Tony, you've got to make this thing work." It was more of a plea for help as opposed to an order.

"Don't worry," I replied with exaggerated bravado, all the while having no clear idea how we'd get it functioning smoothly. (He later became quite a good friend and a mentor.)

I was twenty-nine, and there were half a dozen of us about the same age running the place. We felt a profound sense of responsibility, knowing how dependent the Bank was on us getting it right and making it work. Senior management were lost. This isn't a criticism of Bank leadership, because it was all technical stuff, and they had no idea how to give us direction in terms of what should happen next. Unlike a loan or a mortgage — where they had regulations for the loan and could give clear directions on what we should do and what we shouldn't do — they had no clue in terms of the software, whether it was working and how to move forward.

It was a stimulating project and an exciting time, but it was exhilarating for the wrong reasons. We were less focused on just how groundbreaking or how exciting it was to be working on such a monumental project, and instead we were totally fixated on how to make it work. We never worried that if it didn't work, we'd get fired. But we still felt a huge sense of accountability knowing how much was at stake and how many were dependent upon our being successful. That sense of responsibility stayed with me forever.

In retrospect, the challenges were predictable. (I've since learned that management never fully grasps the cost of complexity.) Naturally, I would say that because I'm a catastrophizer, but also because software in those days was bug-ridden and we felt we had to work all the glitches out before we launched. Today, in smart technology companies, the software is often just as bug-ridden as it ever was in my day. But they don't seek perfection before they release it. Now, because they've got a million people to use and test it, they let their customers do the research. You've seen the updates: "Version 7.2. It fixes this and this and this." There are thousands of bugs in new technology, but because a million people can't get together and just say, "You've got a big problem," they rely on all those individual users to help debug their software.

Bank of Montreal's real-time, national, online software was eventually fixed and working (largely) reliably in 1975, and our department began rebounding to more normal orientation, focusing on daily operations and issues rather than exclusively on crisis management. Around 1977–78, while we were still in the process of rolling out this huge computer system and installing it across the enterprise, the Bank decided they were committed to establishing something called the Systems Steering Committee. The Wild West computer department had entered the mainstream of the business and had to be managed like the rest of it. All the senior executives, including Bill Mulholland (who was the CEO at the time), were on the committee. I was the point man from our technical group, and I'd have to trot over once a month to talk to all the senior executives of the Bank and tell them how we were doing, what was going on with the project, what the issues were and so on.

As the point man on the software project, I got a fair amount of exposure to the senior executives of the Bank. I'll never forget, before one meeting, I was waiting to go in to talk to the Systems Steering Committee about something. I was sitting on the third floor of our head office in Montreal — the turning point of the Bank's universe — and there was an executive committee meeting going on. All the top brass of the Bank were there. As I was waiting for my appointment in the other conference room, Fred McNeil, the Bank's CEO, came out of the executive committee meeting, walked over to me and said, "Tony, congratulations." They had just approved my appointment as vice-president of systems development and that's how I found out. I was becoming an executive at the tender age of thirty-two — the youngest ever at the Bank. So now, after years working with the free spirits in software programming, I had to act like management.

By 1975, Liz and I had been married for four years. We decided to move from downtown Montreal and buy a house in the very east end of Dorval, almost in Lachine. I said, "Liz, we can afford either a house or a car, but not both." So we didn't have a car. That meant late, late at night, after putting in long hours at head office, I'd take the Montreal local bus, which went only as far as 55th Avenue in Lachine. And then I'd walk from there to our house across Lakeshore Boulevard. And in the morning, I would haul my weary bones and walk with Liz up to the corner of our little development to catch the Metropolitan Provincial bus that ran on the Lakeshore at that time of day, and we would both go downtown to work. I think the bus was supposed to come at 7:00 a.m. so we'd be up there at 6:45. Sometimes it would come at 7:00, sometimes earlier, and sometimes not until 7:30. In the middle of winter, we'd be standing there freezing to death.

To keep warm, I bought a lovely warm Hudson's Bay tri-coloured coat. It had a hood and the whole nine yards and was the warmest coat I could find. One day in early 1978, I was in our data centre in Toronto, sitting in a little cubicle. One of the senior vice presidents came in and sat down, saying, "Tony, on Tuesday your name is going to go forward to become an executive with the Bank on one condition."

"What's that?" I asked.

And he says, "You get rid of that #%#@& overcoat!"

Who was I to say no? So that weekend, I went to The Bay and got myself a nice conservative blue coat for my new life as an executive.

Throughout my early career, I kept my head down, fixing problems all over the Bank until I heard the knock on the door in 1990 that signalled I was going to be the chief general manager and chief operating officer — all because I was the catastrophizer. My job was to fix things.

I didn't realize that was what I was all about until after the fact. When Bill Mulholland retired, a couple of us took him out for drinks. He started telling me a story I had never heard from him before, and it was quite revealing. He said, "You know Tony, it's very interesting. Obviously, every job I ever gave you, you did perfectly." (I hadn't realized it was him pulling the strings.) "And it was always the worst, screwed-up situations that we had. I just knew that if I picked up the phone and called you, you were going to do that job well."

My path to the C-suite was circuitous — in my early years at the Bank, it never even crossed my mind that I would ever get there. In hindsight, I learned early on that when everyone else is joining the parade, that's often the best time to re-examine the route map. Healthy skepticism can be a valuable talent against the confirmation bias of others.

And being the catastrophizer had paid off after all.

TONY'S TAKEAWAY

Progress and innovation begin with questioning assumptions. And accepting the challenges you're offered, being true to your talents and instincts and taking responsibility for all the work you do can end up leading to some unexpected places. Being a catastrophizer helps, too.

VOICE: JAMES KELSEY

Jim Kelsey and I have been colleagues and friends at BMO for almost thirty years. I think Jim is the best commercial banker of our generation in our industry. Starting from a lacklustre market position after a decade of rebuilding our risk management function, Jim set out to build what became a truly formidable banking team, leading us to a top-tier market position in less than a decade. The mark of the man and his position with our clients was to have a customer give the lead comments at Jim's retirement celebration.

In my estimation, Tony made a significant contribution in the early 1980s, before he and Matt Barrett took over. The Bank had made a decision in our commercial business to make it difficult for customers that were, say, under $100,000 in borrowing requirements, to do business with us. Essentially, we told them they had to give us the mortgage over their house or get lost. And many of them got lost.

As a result, our market share went from about 17 or 18 percent in the early 1980s down to about 8 percent by 1989. So when Tony and Matt Barrett took over the commercial organization, we had a franchise that was — I don't want to say crumbling, but it had undergone significant negative change. I was appointed to commercial executive in 1989, and with the cooperation, support, encouragement and direction of Tony, Matt, Ron Rogers and Al McNally at the time, we set out a program to bring the market share back. And it took us two, three, four years to go from 8 back to 17 percent.

We regained our position, and at that point we also developed the reputation on the street of being the Maverick Bank. That would've been when Lloyd Atkinson was our chief economist, and we were maybe a half point under the other banks on rates, which was unheard of at the time. So it was a strategy that worked very well for us. We also had a smaller book than the other banks, so offering a cheaper rate hurt us less than it might have hurt the other guys.

So I would say that was probably one of the defining moments where I thought that leadership coming from the top — people like Tony — played an integral part in the Bank recovering. Today, commercial is still the bread and butter, from a profitability point of view, both north and south of the border. The commercial franchise is the Bank, and we would have a hard time keeping up if we hadn't had such a strong franchise.

CHAPTER 6

Leadership Is Selling Your Ideas

Earn what you can since everything's for sale.
— GEOFFREY CHAUCER, *The Canterbury Tales*

The great baseball manager Casey Stengel was once asked the secret to managing. "Managing," said Casey, "is keeping the five guys in the room who hate your guts away from the five guys who haven't made up their mind yet." I think Stengel had it right. Over my forty years at BMO — and since then as well — I've been asked by hundreds of people, including lots of young people, about leadership. "What do you think is the most important skill a leader should have?"

While my response is not as pithy as Casey's, I think it makes a necessary point: "Interpersonal skills in general, and specifically selling your ideas." You may not realize it, but absolutely everybody, and not just in banks, but *everybody* in the universe, is basically in a sales job. We're all selling. We're selling our ideas. We're selling our goals. We're selling our feelings. Everything is a sales job.

Getting people to see the whole picture means selling them on your vision. I saw John Cleese recently, and he was brilliant. I mean, it was not only funny, but illuminating. He said only 10 to 15 percent of the people in any profession know what the hell they're doing — the rest are bystanders. He argued that competence and confidence are inversely correlated.

If you ask any CEO, in any organization, anywhere in the world, "What would you like to have done better when you were CEO?" the person would probably say, "I should have moved more quickly on personnel changes." Namely, getting rid of underperformers. When you get into a really senior position, it's too easy to just leave things as is, to *not* clean house. No matter how long and how hard you try, some people will never agree with sweeping HR changes. Leadership comes with that clarity of vision. And motivating others to move the organization along in the right direction means selling everyone on your vision for it, whatever that may be.

How you get through to them is crucial. Admittedly, calling it *salesmanship* is a bit oversimplified, I know. So I sometimes use the term *interpersonal skills* instead of *selling*, because you don't get things done — in this era in particular — by yelling at colleagues or telling them what to do. You get things done by persuading them, by leading them to your goals. Selling them on your ideas. Managing a bank — or any organization — is a people business. Staff want to believe your goals are their goals. Sell them on your ability to get them there. That's my idea of leadership.

I may be a catastrophizer by nature, but my profession isn't a banker; it's a salesperson. That's my skill. And it underpinned my leadership style, such as it is, in the departments I led and the people I hired.

In fact, you can take all this one step further: using your influence and interpersonal skills to sell people on your vision is all about using your emotional intelligence to manage relationships. I had an advantage in my leadership at the Bank because I had institutional memory. I could walk into any room or any situation and know, for example, that I'd started there as a messenger in my teens. That I'd already seen most of the things new employees were likely to see and more. That I'd trotted securities up and down Bay Street and had come by my knowledge honestly, because of the background that I had gained by working for six years in fairly low-level jobs. By telling staff these anecdotes, I usually got their attention. And I always tell them, when you've seen as much of the business as I have — in so many roles and from so many perspectives — leadership *all* boils down to managing relationships.

Other than that, I don't think I ever had a defined leadership style. My philosophy was that I never believed in giving a lot of direction; managing people is not about micromanaging them. I preferred to say broadly, *Here are our goals, our objectives. Here are the guidelines of what it's all about. You've got a job you were hired to do; now, go ahead and do it.* I believe in treating people as equals and partners, as colleagues — not as subordinates to my role as boss.

I certainly didn't set out in my first management job to articulate a particular leadership philosophy, but over the course of a forty-year career I've sort of developed my own guiding rules. Many of these insights were won the hard way — figuring things out on the job, sometimes making mistakes — but they always propelled me in my career, and they seemed to work for my staff and my colleagues.

RULE 1: Fit First

Although my first real management job was in the human resources department, I believe that an overreliance on organizational HR designs, despite all of the wonderful purposes they serve, can get in the way of doing what I think is one of the most important things from a talent management perspective: making sure that people are in the right slot in your organization.

HR processes can certainly support good hiring practices, but when you're in a leadership position, you are the one who makes a selection about the right person to do the job. Once you've made the decision, now you're responsible. It's not HR's job to manage that human resource; it's yours. My theory is to pick somebody you believe is capable of doing the job and then recognize they're an adult and they deserve to be treated accordingly.

Now, this kind of relatively unstructured manager-employee relationship raises the obvious question: What about accountability, and what happens if somebody doesn't do the job? Well, that becomes apparent soon enough, and then you can deal with it in one of two ways. You can call them on their performance and tell them to shape up; generally, however, that's not going to work, because if they have a poor attitude, you can't change that attitude simply by pointing it out to them. Which leads to my second technique: you deal with the under-performance head-on, which I will explain more in Rule 3.

RULE 2: Don't Let Management Processes Manage You

Another thing about HR policies and procedures is that they can take on a life of their own or take over completely. They can also become a crutch for managers who don't really want to manage their people. I recall my misgivings about the formal, written performance appraisal system. While I understand the need for large organizations to have uniform administrative personnel assessment processes, they can also have unintended and negative effects. I used to counsel managers who reported to me, "Don't let the written performance-appraisal process do your managing for you." In my opinion, this process is useful for managing the salary budget, and I acknowledge that you must have policies — particularly in large companies. But the formal appraisal process can turn people into amateur psychologists despite the fact that most people are not good at it. They generally do a lousy job and end up taking shortcuts intellectually when judging people. And people can game the system.

I remember an assessment of my own that illustrates this very point. When I was in the technology department, far from reaching the VP level, I was still a young guy and sure of myself. The boss had to do my performance appraisal and the categories were, "Low competent, unsatisfactory, competent, high competent, excellent." Nobody ever got excellent. If you were really good you got high competent; if you were okay you got competent. Nobody managed to get low competent either, because managers didn't have the nerve to give such a low appraisal, which is yet another reason why I hate this system.

In my assessment situation, the boss brought me in and had written me up as competent. I was shocked. "What do you mean competent?" I asked. "This is depressing. I've never been rated lower than high competent in my entire Bank career."

But he'd been rehearsing this, you see. His one killer line was, "Tony, you should hope that you're never in a job long enough to get rated higher than competent." In other words, don't stagnate long enough to get that good at any one job.

I acknowledge that, in general, it takes time for an individual to achieve full competence or above in many jobs — and increasingly so in more senior jobs. But this way of thinking fails to acknowledge employees with exceptional ability who can master jobs in a short period — these are the ones we should value.

In my view, an informal dialogue with people is a far more productive way of assessing performance and providing feedback than sitting in a stiff, formal setting and just following a protocol. In my observation, the really smart people are much harder on themselves than you could ever be on them. So sometimes, for the really good people and the high performers, part of your role as their manager is to pump them up, because they tend to be really harsh on themselves and self-critical. It's the same in companies, the same on sports teams. That's hard to do when you're hobbled by a system that doesn't allow you to give top marks to top performers.

RULE 3: Manage Underperformers

Unfortunately, it's usually the lower performers who think they're stars, and that's an issue that's much more difficult to deal with. Most leaders will go with the team that's in place when they step into their role, until they figure out, "Hey, we can make it happen without Charlie."

I've always felt that as a leader you have to condition yourself to deal with those underperformers, and most don't. They shuffle them around and make them someone else's problem. You can often tell an underperformer very quickly by how often they've had a job change within an organization.

My philosophy is if you keep that failing person, you're not doing them any favours. Either they don't have the skills you thought they had, they don't have the motivation or something else is going on in their life. You're doing them and the organization a disservice by keeping them on. They could wind up at age fifty-five having to come to grips with the fact they were never suited for the job they'd taken thirty years earlier, and nobody had ever told them. You've got to give them a chance to start somewhere else, maybe in a different role, maybe doing something different with a different company or a different boss.

When I was advising managers on how to deal with underperformers I would say, "You have to consider that you're doing them a favour, and you're doing the organization a favour. Because if somebody is under-performing in this job, it doesn't mean they're a bad person; it's just that their skillset doesn't match up with whatever it is we want to do. Let's not get into attitude, because then you're playing junior psychologist. Just conclude that it's a skillset issue. And if we just keep moving them around without addressing that mismatch, they're going to lose five, seven, ten years out of their career when they could be getting into something they're good at and making a contribution."

This is why I disliked policies where you can't really dismiss somebody. Some companies shift them to another department and fabricate an excuse about why they're doing it to avoid handing out criticism. Such a lateral move is pointless, because if they're not doing a job correctly, it's not necessarily their fault as an individual; it could be that their values and talents don't align with the organization's mission and goals. Or it could be a culture thing — sometimes it just won't work out if the fit isn't there (see Rule 1). It's far better to recognize the issue, deal with it promptly and cut the tie right there.

Some might say this is all self-serving and a little cold. But it was always very difficult for me to let people go. It affected me deeply, because I believe I am a compassionate person, and I've always been interested in helping others and accomplishing things as a team. I think it's safe to say that most leaders have an aversion to letting people go — no one likes to do it. But the way to think about it, and this is not a rationalization, is that in the end you're doing a better thing for them as well as for the organization. You're doing a bad thing for everyone if you fail to step up to reality.

RULE 4: Engage People

I'm not so taken with the concept of the management meeting where you corral everybody and put them into a big room, and you stand at the front pitching them all on why the latest business plan, initiative or outlook for the year is a wonderful thing. Everybody in the audience, even the top performers, are sitting there with eyes glazing over as you're doing the sheep dip trying to convince them why the business plan is wonderful. Pretty soon they lose interest, their minds wander and they're thinking about what they'll have for dinner that night.

The bigger issue is that drinking your own Kool-Aid all the time without input from other people is counter to productivity and performance. Talking at people is lecturing, and it's the surest way to lose them. In other words, you need to engage the people who work for you to harness their talent, differences, expertise and experience in order to solve problems more effectively, innovate and achieve the organization's goals. Your job as a leader is to show them the vision, inspire them to believe in it and empower them to achieve it.

One of my top ten non-fiction books is *How We Know What Isn't So: The Fallibility of Human Reason in Everyday Life,* by Thomas Gilovich. It's a book about statistics and the author starts off by talking about the theory of the hot hand in basketball. People believe, "Oh, this guy shot four three-pointers in a row. He's going to get the fifth one for sure. He's got a hot hand." Which, of course, is absolute nonsense; there's no such thing as a hot hand. Using regression to the norm, the author demonstrates statistically why that notion is complete rubbish. Even statisticians fall into this trap.

This is what Daniel Kahneman shows in his book *Thinking, Fast and Slow.* Anyone who is an expert in their own profession is at risk of believing their own infallibility to the point where they can't even accept outside information. We want to believe what we think we know. Kahneman calls it the Illusion of Validity (a term coined in a 1973 paper he co-authored with Amos Tversky). When we leap to conclusions, which we all do, what we think we know can easily be not so. It's essential to empower the people who work for you not only to make their own valuable contributions, but also to challenge you and your assumptions. That leads to better outcomes for everyone and for the organization.

When I was hiring, particularly in technology, I had a huge proclivity to hire engineers. I loved engineers, because these men and women are basically problem-solvers — they don't necessarily operate from a book. They use deduction and reasoning, and they question everything. They're open to new ways of doing things. They're the kind of people you want showing up at nine o'clock on Monday morning when your quarterly results have just gone in the tank because some bozo lent money to someone he never should have.

I love problem-solvers. Let me give you an example that has nothing to do with banking. One of my favourite writers is Atul Gawande. He's a surgeon and has written some brilliant books on the medical field — *The Checklist Manifesto, Complications, Being Mortal* — as well as articles in *The New Yorker*. One of his subjects is the huge rate today of methicillin-resistant staphylococcus aureus (MRSA) and other staph bacteria in hospitals. And it's pretty frightening that we don't hear about it enough. These life-threatening antibiotic-resistant bacteria are all over, and no matter what you go in the hospital for, you have a high likelihood of contracting an infection thanks to one of them.

The most common precaution was to spray all surfaces liberally with chemicals and disinfectants, but Gawande thinks there's a specific reason for the spread of MRSA and similar bacteria. His analysis in *The Checklist Manifesto* reveals that it's not just the microbes in play; there's a cultural phenomenon that proliferates their spread. His point is that if you go into an operating room, who's the boss? The surgeons. They're gods. And they have a bunch of nurses who are the "plebs." And so, God forbid the nurses ever tell the surgeons what to do or not to do. "Excuse me. I'm the surgeon. I'm in charge here."

Gawande observed that a lot of the incidences of these deadly infectious diseases were reportedly coming from basic things like unclean hands, due in no small part to surgeons not following the correct protocol of handwashing and sanitization (a process that foreshadowed the hand-washing practices during the COVID-19 pandemic). So, he explained, the only way he was going to change this at the hospital where he worked was to change the culture, to empower everybody in the operating room as equals and to empower everyone to speak up. And he was going to train them to encourage this culture change. He called this "The Checklist Manifesto." So the nurses can say to the surgeon, "You didn't wash your hands just after doing that procedure, before taking up that instrument." And the surgeon would learn that it's acceptable to follow her order rather than making her feel like she's going to be in trouble for daring to speak to a superior in such a way.

Once this "Checklist Manifesto" was working at many hospitals, the MRSA incidents at those hospitals went to virtually zero. *Zero.* He's written up his work with clinical therapist Dr. Peter Pronovost in *The New Yorker* and elsewhere. This brilliant medical breakthrough is also an excellent cultural insight for organizations: it had nothing to do with antiseptics and soaps and everything to do with engaging and empowering your talent to speak up, to challenge authority and assumptions and to contribute.

RULE 5: Focus on Results, Not on How You Get There

I've always managed to objectivize results. Not punching the clock was part of that. When I was running the technology group, removing the punch clock was particularly important because people in that department are not showing up at nine o'clock in the morning and working until five o'clock. Furthermore, that's not what the organization requires of them when there's a crisis to be managed; you need them there when you need them, not according to some arbitrary workday schedule.

One of our great software programmers would routinely work at night, and he'd stay all night long. He'd come in anywhere between seven o'clock and ten o'clock at night, wearing track pants and sporting his long beard, and he'd work until about six o'clock in the morning, because he didn't want other people around. That's when you want to work? Fine. Why do I care? Just show me the product. He was a brilliant software developer, and he was eight times more productive than a lot of the other programmers.

Other people in our knowledge business saw that and said, "Well, why am I doing nine to five? Why am I on a treadmill while you are letting him do that?" And I would say, "Did I say you had to work from nine to five? No." I had no problem with allowing flexibility as long as it produced the results we were after. The same rule applied to my assistant Nancy. If she took time out of the workday because she had an appointment at one o'clock in the afternoon, I was fine with that, because she would then break her neck to make up for it and would pitch in when she was needed in an emergency, sometimes staying until ten o'clock at night because something had to get done right away. The results are what matters — not face time.

Sometimes it's only the illusion of face time. One thing I learned when I was involved with the advancement of women program (more on that in Chapter 12) is that one of the entirely fallacious knocks on women in the workplace was that they left precisely at five o'clock because they had children they had to get home to. Some people pointed out, "We work really hard all day. We stay late, and they don't." However, what those very people (almost always men) did was put their jackets on the back of their chair and leave to play squash from 5 till 7:30 p.m., have a couple of drinks and then come back. But the jackets were always on the chairs while they were doing that. So the bosses would think, "Oh they're still here and working; they must be hard workers."

The same people who were complaining about women only showing up between nine and five were preserving only the image of face time. Of course, although the women weren't in the office before and after business hours (or leaving their jackets there pretending to be at work) they'd usually still be working, on the phone, on the computer and emailing clients — all while looking after their kids.

Coming back to being a catastrophizer, I'll confess that my nature was driven by my obsessive compulsive disorder (OCD). Constantly believing that something is going to go wrong has always been a millstone I carry and still is to this day. *What's going to go wrong with this thing? What's going to go wrong with this plan? What is going to go wrong with this approach?* This kind of constant catastrophic thinking doesn't make life easy; but, paradoxically, I think it has served me well as a leader. The trick was to avoid spinning my wheels and instead turn my obsessive worrying into creative solutions and problem-solving and even into positive leadership behaviour.

My relentless questioning was fantastic for problem-solving at the Bank and for healthy, productive working relationships with employees. Every day someone would come to me and say, "We're going to do *this*."

My natural response would be, "Well, what happens if *this* doesn't work?"

"That's not going to happen."

So then I followed up with the inevitable flood of questions: "Well, how do you know? And what if it *does* go wrong? I don't care whether it does or doesn't, but what would you do if it did? What's your contingency plan for this kind of thing failing? And if you don't have one then you haven't really thought your way through it, because how are you going to respond to things not going according to plan?"

What I came to realize over time is that my catastrophizing actually helped me engage with the people who reported to me. They felt like I was interested in their work, actively listening to their ideas. And I was naturally encouraging scenario planning and creative solutions. Trust me, I didn't have an alternative, because that's just the way that I am. But the point is I was behaving as an authentic leader, bringing my true self to work and tapping into it to achieve my goals and the organization's goals, and to guide my relationships with colleagues.

TONY'S TAKEAWAY

Banking is a people business, and so are most enterprises. Customers and employees alike want to believe your goals are their goals. Sell them on your ability to get them there. You may not be a catastrophizer yourself, but the golden rule of leadership is to be true to yourself, to be authentic. Know thyself and lead accordingly, follow my five fundamental rules, and everything else will fall into place.

VOICE: **BARRY GILMOUR**

Barry Gilmour is highly respected in the IT industry and was a valued member of the Bank's senior management team. In time he succeeded my role as CIO piloting our bank through several phases of digital automation innovations. Barry and I have been friends and colleagues for almost forty years.

Over forty years ago, I replaced Tony in a job where he'd been the youngest executive ever in the Bank. He was something of a boy wonder if you will, at that stage. I was an outside hire, brought in at a fairly senior level to step into his shoes and fit into the organization. It was an interesting relationship, following along behind him for a little while. After a time, we also became good friends.

One thing that brought us together was the respect I had for him as an individual. A lot of that was driven not only by his smarts — he is *extremely* smart — but also, more importantly, by his integrity. To me that was a key thing. I've often said to people, "If you're really lucky, you can count your real friends on one hand. I doubt you're going to get past five, to be quite honest." I'm talking about *real* friends as opposed to good acquaintances and all the rest of that. I personally would say I have three true friends, of which Tony is one. And they all share a lot of the same characteristics: mostly, the relationships I have with them are all driven by integrity and respect.

Tony is an avid reader. I remember at one stage walking into his office for a meeting and he started with, "If I read three books a week for the rest of my life, I'm going to read only — " whatever that worked out to — 2,500 or 3,000. "And that's not acceptable." Another great characteristic is that he's very open-minded, which is probably part of why he's continuously learning and still taking courses to this day.

Tony has a bit of a self-effacing nature and unlike many people he recognizes his own limitations. He made sure he knew of other people's strengths and weaknesses and tried to complement them with his own, such that the whole would be greater than the sum of the parts. For example, he doesn't really seek conflict, shall we say? But on an intellectual level, he'll go at it all the time, no problem whatsoever. By contrast, I would call Matt Barrett and myself street fighters. I don't have any problem throwing elbows, never did. I don't think Matt really did either, to be honest. So their contrast in styles was complementary — and good for the Bank.

I remember Tony saying to me very early on in my career, "If there's one piece of advice I could give you, it would be, before you say anything, count to ten and think about it (whatever *it* is), and then say what you're thinking. It's not that what you say immediately is wrong, but sometimes it'll come across better if you're seen to be giving it a bit more thought." I don't think I ever got past seven without realizing he was right. What else can I say, he's just genuinely a nice guy.

CHAPTER 7

Change Is Hard:
Success Can Take a Lifetime

People can die of mere imagination.
— GEOFFREY CHAUCER, *The Canterbury Tales*

One of my earliest lessons in business and most closely held beliefs is that it takes a long time to change a corporate culture. One of the examples I like to cite is one where two car manufacturers merge. The two principals of the deal are being interviewed, and it's going well, until one of the CEOs is asked, "How long do you think it's going to take before the two companies really come together, before the cultures merge?"

"Forty-three years," he replies with certainty.

"Why do you say forty-three years?"

"That's when the last of us in the top jobs in these two companies will be dead."

That might be a little dramatic. But culture is so deeply ingrained in many organizations that it stays forever in the people who work there. That's the problem with mergers, in general: the dealmakers often underestimate the time it takes to change a way of doing things. In my years at the Bank, I had many opportunities to experience exactly this culture phenomenon. Why is it important? If you can't sell your employees on your culture how are you going to get customers to buy in?

One of my favourite takeaways from technology innovations in banking is that people in general are resistant to change in your culture — not only the employees who are living the consequences of change in the organization, but also the general public. Most people are resistant to change and adapt to it very slowly. When our marketing guys are interviewing customers, saying, "Do you use online banking and the other technology-enabled services we offer?" most will answer, "Oh, yeah, sure. I'm right in there with all that." But they aren't telling the whole truth. There are always the early adopters, of course, but most don't take to new technology that quickly.

So I suppose we shouldn't have been surprised at the slow buy-in from the public on the banking terminals BMO started introducing in the mid-'70s (they weren't called ATMs or ABMs till the mid-'80s). They seem so normal today, and even old-fashioned compared to online banking and depositing cheques via cell phone, for example, but it took ages for these automated banking machines to catch on with customers.

We installed the first Instabank in 1975 in Montreal. The Toronto implementation would have been not that long after that, probably 1976. I want to say the first one was in the Manulife Centre — that would have been a logical place for it: central Toronto, Bay and Bloor, a pretty big branch, sophisticated clientele, a lot of university kids. But ABMs didn't become ubiquitously used until a number of years later. My rule was that each ABM had to do, on average, three hundred transactions a day to make them cost-effective for the Bank. And would you believe that to get to three hundred transactions a day per machine across the entire network of ABMs probably took until 1990? They were an overnight sensation that took almost twenty years to succeed.

Why? First, those machines were a headache at the beginning — the migraine of all time. They worked less often than they didn't in the earliest days. But even more difficult was getting people to try them. When we installed the ones at First Canadian Place and elsewhere, we'd have to take one of the tellers and put them right next to the machine. As the customers would be going to line up for a teller at the counter, the employee at the ABM would buttonhole them and say, "Tired of standing in line? Let me show you how easy it is to use this machine!" It took that kind of energy and hands-on customer support every day for years to change people's habits and gain wide acceptance for the Instabank machines. And even in the age of online banking, we're still not completely there with the ABMs.

As an aside, the irony about them is that they were not originally seen by the Bank as primarily designed for the needs of customers. This enterprise-wide automation began initially as a productivity improvement, reducing the number of tellers we employed and streamlining our operations. That was the whole thinking behind it. Any-branch banking? It enabled productivity by freeing up tellers to do more useful work. The fact that the public liked the convenience of being able to use any Bank of Montreal branch to deposit and withdraw was a nice add-on idea. We had created a system that was capable of doing this, but that wasn't the entire purpose.

Anyway, how slow is the process of getting customers to change their habits? Fast forward to 2018. My friend Enzo said to me, "I was walking our dog Tessa to the Manulife branch as I normally do. It's on my route, and I took her to see your niece, Katie, who usually pats the dog and we chat. But she was busy today with an older man who had been in the line to cash a cheque or do something at the teller. As I was watching, Katie took him over to the automated banking machine and took the time to show him how to use it so he wouldn't have to stand in line for the teller anymore. He was overjoyed! He'd never had the experience, but she took time out to show him." Remember, this was in 2018 — and we had started installing ABMs in 1975! We are *still* having to work at changing people's banking habits, even as the technology continues to evolve around them.

Change requires more than patience to be successful: the timing also has to be right. For example, we launched m_banx back in 1996 as a stand-alone system for internet banking. The idea of trusting your banking to an online source outside your branch was way ahead of its time, and it met resistance. The public wasn't ready for this particular innovation when the internet itself was in the embryonic stage. They had to get used to the World Wide Web in general before they could take to our specific application of it. Eventually all the banks integrated internet banking into their regular, branch-based services.

But none of this is new. Major technological advances in banking have been going on for thirty-five or forty years. It wasn't always at the pace it happens now, and maybe it's a little more noticeable today; when you actually knock the branch down because so much of the business is automated or has migrated online, customers tend to notice that something's happened to change banking as they know it.

Even the Bank itself, as an organization, is resistant to change. And the senior leadership team — the changemakers at the top — are sometimes not that easy to convince. Change is risky and it's hard for everyone. My old boss in the technology department, Bob MacDougall, understood that. But he also knew that getting away from the old regionally based data-gathering systems — with their time lag of overnight updates — to a national, real-time system to communicate information would be a very powerful marketing idea. Customers would always know instantly what their account balances were, what transactions they'd done and so on. He knew that, but that's not how we justified the installation initially to the board or to the executives. It was all productivity improvement, reducing the numbers of tellers while allowing us to expand other services we provided. We focused on internal workings of the organization — the things they knew — the financial benefits to the Bank and on bottom-line results. Everyone could understand that without too much imagination.

That leads me to a sidebar. All software is complex and everybody — senior management especially — just wants the technology behind any change to be done instantaneously. They believe it's the panacea for making change happen smoothly and seamlessly. That's human nature, says Austin Adams, formerly Chief Information Officer at America's three largest banks. When I asked him about this issue he told me, "Interestingly, while some 'C'-level executives were interested in the direct and indirect cost of numbers of systems and related issues, the only consistent message that resonated was their understanding of how speed to market with new product was being slowed by multiple products, support to maintain those systems and lack of a streamlined approach to product development." Getting management to move away from such biases is another of the challenges that make culture change so stubborn

There's a lot of discussion about artificial intelligence these days and all the problems it will be able to solve. There is no question that computer software has become incredibly sophisticated in its function and its ability to replace or support human activity. But my personal view is that we vastly underestimate the sophistication of the human brain. I believe the most modern software still remains short of the human brain's capability. While others might disagree, I believe it'll be many years before it comes close.

Aware of my interest in research on information technology, Harvard professor Nicholas G. Carr interviewed me for his book *Does IT Matter?* In one section, I spoke about why a lot of what we develop in IT is resisted by the staff, sharing an example from when we put together the online banking system at BMO. Its functionality was unprecedented, covering and facilitating just about any procedure we could think of that the tellers might need to do. I think there were something like three hundred to four hundred different permutations and combinations of transactions, and they now had them all at their fingertips.

Typically, however, tellers used about eight different types of transactions routinely. So, instead of riffling through all the manuals to find the very limited number of functions they do all the time, they would create crib notes of the five or six things they use all the time, write them down and Scotch-tape that list to the front of the teller terminal. This, after all the technology that we had spent millions of dollars developing and the enormous functionality we had built into the system? How much of a waste is that? But the tellers stuck to what they knew they needed rather than learn and explore the new, advanced and comprehensive support system we had designed for them.

Change is emotional, so people resist it. But corporate cultures do survive it and so does the general public. And it's not going to stop anytime soon, so we all need to know how to manage it. For instance, those ABM machines we struggled so hard to integrate with our customers will become different machines in the future. They'll become more sophisticated, with more interactive capabilities that will start to take up more and more of even the "relationship" business that goes on at the branches. Even now you can see that. All the banks have an interactive capability on the ABMs. When the technology evolves, and when the market's ready and the consumers are ready, you'll see ABMs move away from distributing cash and printing statements. Already they're experimenting in different places. Japan is probably ahead of everybody on this.

Some wonder if this spells the end of the branch. But in 2018 there were still 5,578 branches for the Big Six banks combined. That's only about 2.9 percent fewer than a decade earlier. Canada had twenty branches for every 100,000 adults as of 2018, down from about twenty-five per 100,000 adults before the 2008 financial crisis, according to the World Bank. Still, that's more than some predicted there would be. Our CFO Tom Flynn was quoted by Bloomberg, saying he expects a gradual decline in both the number of branches and their average size amid a continued push towards digital banking. BMO had 891 domestic locations as of 2019, which generated about C$9 million in annual sales on average, a 55 percent jump in sales from 2009. The long term impact of COVID-19 on those numbers won't be known for years.

Although there is less need for many of the banking services we thought were so important back in the 1970s (such as cheque-cashing, cash dispensing and so on), there still is a huge need on the relationship end of the business to help people think about how they are doing financially and what they are doing to improve their financial situation: Are they going to buy a house or make an investment? What do they do if their mother has died without having made a will? Will the province take over and run the estate? Are her financial affairs a mess? Who's there to put their arms around them when they're facing major life changes and decisions about money?

Today, the branch has become an office of people who can provide advice and help — the whole relationship end of the business. That part of the business will never be automated because it's too complex and you need that relationship between the individuals, customers and advisors. The vast network of branches that were necessary to support a transaction-heavy business? Gone. But the intelligent migration is to use some of that physical real estate to house people who have a broader skill set and information base to fulfill that relationship role, whether it's investing or helping customers through life-cycle events. And, for the time being, even a reduced branch network serves another priority of the business: having physical locations gives the company an identity and a presence in the communities in which it serves. (We'll talk more about branding later in the book, in Chapter 15.)

In retrospect, there has been a sea change in banking culture and technology over the forty years of my career. It all looks very ordered now and, looking back, people think there was a steady progress on both these fronts over the years. But we had our hands full, and who knew when we were working on the systems for the first ABMs in the 1970s that we'd still have employees showing customers how to use the machines today? But that's how long it can take to change a culture.

To manage change in all aspects of its business, the Bank has come more and more to rely on problem-solvers like me. When I was a lowly programmer trying to come up with a technology solution every time we hit a wall, I couldn't know that change management is what I'd be doing on a grand scale throughout my career, particularly as a senior executive. But, ultimately, it did turn out well in my case.

What has always struck me when I think about change in corporate cultures is that such profound responsibility was given to me as a fairly junior guy, operating on the cutting edge of the software development that was so new at the time and would become so central to the Bank evolving over the years. And that has stuck with me to this day.

TONY'S TAKEAWAY

All the changemakers among us, and particularly the leaders of change, have a responsibility to move innovation forward without rocking people's worlds too dramatically. Remember, overnight success is often a lengthy process. Be prepared for a marathon — not a sprint — when cultures collide.

VOICE: **ROB PRICHARD** oc, **PART 1**

Rob Prichard and I first met when he was a newly elected president of University of Toronto and I was a newly appointed Ontario government appointee to the university's governing council. Our collaboration was both effective and a pleasure. I became chair of the governing council and then with Rob, chair of the Capital Campaign for the University of Toronto, the largest private-sector campaign in Canadian history. In my view Rob was the best president of the University of Toronto, certainly in my memory and experience. During his ten years as president, U of T's endowment rose to $1.4 billion, the most of any Canadian university. Through my inducement, Rob joined BMO's board upon retirement from the university and subsequently was chosen by his fellow directors to be chair of BMO's board.

When I was president of the University of Toronto from 1990 to 2000 — and before I joined the board of BMO — Tony was chair of the university's governing council, a large board of fifty members with overall fiduciary responsibility for the university. The role of chairman is a demanding job marked by many meetings, many stakeholders and many time demands. Tony was also the bridge between the council and the university's administration, which I led. He did a terrific job as chair, served four years in the role, was always available with wise counsel and somehow managed to do his day job at the bank at the same time.

We were planning a major fundraising campaign for the university, seeking $350 million, the largest campaign ever launched among Canadian universities at the time. A critical question was who we should invite to lead the campaign, knowing it was an essential but demanding role that would be a key to our success. One summer day, Tony's wife, Elizabeth, called me at our cottage. She knew we were struggling with the question, and she suggested we invite Tony to serve — a prospect that had never crossed my mind since he was already carrying such a heavy load. However, I took Liz's call as evidence that they had discussed it and that if asked, Tony would serve. I asked him, he agreed to serve and the rest is history.

Under Tony's leadership, the university not only met the $350 million goal but raised it twice over and in the end was the first campaign in Canadian history to raise over $1 billion. It was a masterful performance by Tony, who provided steady and determined leadership, greatly strengthening the university and raising the bar for Canadian philanthropy as a whole. I know of no other university board chair who has simultaneously also led that university's major fundraising campaign, much less one of historic scale. After completing his service as chair of the governing council and his leadership of the campaign, Tony was awarded an honorary Doctor of Laws degree from U of T — one of the most richly deserved in the university's long history.

CHAPTER 8

Centralized Corporations and the Cost of Complexity

Patience is a conquering virtue.
— GEOFFREY CHAUCER

A ustin Adams, whom I introduced before, is a brilliant friend of mine whose insights on IT have led him to be Chief Information Officer at First Union which became JPMorgan Chase, Bank One, and Wells Fargo. His experience spans the growth of IT from its infancy to being at the core of today's complex world. Upon his retirement in 2006, I asked him how tech leaders could better do their jobs. Adams told me, "Our greatest opportunity for improvement would be to help CEOs, COOs and CFOs better understand the cost of complexity.

"I believe tech leaders are uniquely positioned to see the complexity of not only the numbers of tech systems, standards, architecture, etc., but perhaps more importantly, the number of business-driven decisions that add to burdensome complexity. That is, the number of products, reporting systems, project methodologies, unnecessary geographical differences, etc. The greatest of which many times are driven by management ego and turf issues."

Better than anything I could say, Austin sums up the challenges facing today's CEO grappling with IT. One perennial debate that interests me — and which has never been resolved — is the question of centralization versus decentralization within a corporation. Which is the better philosophy to adopt? If you're an operations person, like me, productivity means centralization. But if you're an executive running a separate business division within a corporation, decentralization is probably preferred, and you resist every attempt to become part of the bigger entity. You run your own thing, because — although there's a lot to be said for all of us working together as a team — you don't want to be absorbed by the broader culture. One wants unity and uniformity and the other wants independence. That debate has gone on forever in organizations.

I saw it firsthand. As I've described in earlier chapters, when the information technology revolution struck, one of my first big breaks came when I joined Operations and Systems in 1970. With the support of the Bank, I changed careers. I went back to school to become an IT professional and emerged six months later as a computer programmer. I quickly became immersed in the development of our nationwide online banking system, which — some people forget — was revolutionary at the time. No one else in banking was doing it in Canada or the United States.

I still shake my head when I say this, but I was one of the people who helped develop the computer system that allowed us to engage in real-time banking across six time zones. That was not something, to paraphrase Hamlet, "dreamt of in my philosophies." I spent just over a decade in Operations, where I earned my first vice-presidency, and where I would do a second stint, this time as the executive vice-president in charge, just prior to being appointed president in 1990.

For the IT professionals with whom I worked at the Bank in the early 1970s, computer-based support for banking transactions and passbook updating came by way of applications that were run at IBM and other service bureaus. We supplied them with data, which they accumulated and turned around. It was anything but instantaneous. But then, with a little help from technology, in-house computers and IT programmers, the Bank helped change the economics and the approach. The advent of decentralized IT was the result.

Technology trailblazer Gordon Moore predicted that computing would dramatically increase in power, and decrease in relative cost, at an exponential pace. The insight, known as Moore's Law, became the golden rule for the electronics industry, and a springboard for innovation. And, of course, Moore's prediction came true, leading ultimately to more computing power in an inexpensive watch than in the mainframes that we used to provide nationwide online banking in 1975.

As costs dropped in computing, as happened to all technologies, the era of the so-called minicomputer dawned, making it possible for business units or departments within the larger corporate environment to acquire and install computer technology in the business unit or departments. Business units began to recruit "their own" computer programmers to develop and maintain "their own" applications to support the business, without input from the centralized units.

To back up a second, when business units begin to establish their own IT units, it struck a discordant note in me. First, computers were still very expensive devices in the scheme of office equipment. Replicating them in every unit would be very costly. Second, top-tier IT professionals were still a scarce resource, and while we could attract the best and most skilled to work on large-scale equipment solving business-wide problems, smaller business units would be less likely to attract top-tier talent. Worse, business-unit managers, underskilled at IT, wouldn't appreciate or be able to assess the capabilities of their small standalone IT functions, or the professionals they had hired to staff them. In the valley of the blind, the one-eyed man is king!

As business units made decisions on how to staff their decentralized IT needs, the issue from a corporate perspective became efficiency versus effectiveness. How to best achieve distribution of the resources while still inspiring the creativity of smaller units? Should you have one large, centralized IT unit or a series of smaller decentralized ones? It was less efficient for a corporation to have a costly archipelago of IT departments, each with an expensive set of resources. At best the distributed resources would be a second-tier solution to a business-unit problem. They would be differently replicated to solve similar business problems in various business units — with none being the most effective solution to a common problem.

A common solution to the same problem within the entire company would be more effective. Of course, the argument for effectiveness of business units having "their own" resources — best to have decision-making close to those affected — had some credence. But when you then added the necessity of support and maintenance, the argument for decentralization lost a lot of its steam.

As I moved up in the organization, I observed similar issues of efficiency and effectiveness with other support functions — satellite libraries, for instance. They were springing up with sub-optimal purchasing power and duplication. The same debate ensued about distributed financial analysis and control functions and distributed human resource functions. How to find a balance between the needs of the business units and the interests of the organization as a whole? In response to the business-unit complaint that centralized support functions were unresponsive to the needs of individual profit centres, we developed a hybrid model, distributing highly skilled resources that jointly "belonged" to both the business unit and the governing central function. This allowed us to be creative in our decision-making and problem-solving yet maintain the strong controls essential to running a major financial institution in Canada. I believe that this hybrid centralized-decentralized model made us stronger, more innovative and more resilient as an organization.

For one, our hybrid model enabled staff in the individual business units to provide feedback and solutions from the frontlines to the centralized functions. It was exactly this kind of two-way information flow that allowed for a key innovation in our nascent online banking system and improved our centrally controlled security systems — and led to one of my favourite examples of how our distributed model enhanced creativity in our problem-solving and decision-making throughout the Bank.

Because banks are always concerned about security and privacy, people believed the open-banking concept with terminals in the branches (and eventually available to individual customers online) was never going to go anywhere. How could you secure the system? Ours was going to be radically different in inventive ways, which I still love to this day.

When updating all transactions, including passbooks for savings accounts, we printed out information using an IBM Selectric typewriter. You may not remember, but the IBM Selectric typewriter that emerged in 1961 was quite ingenious for the time. As opposed to having individual clackety-clack keys on separate bars that had characterized typewriters forever, the Selectric had one single ball with all the characters on it. It was quiet and it was faster. We could very quickly and automatically update customers' passbooks by printing all their transactions from the system on small individual sheets of paper that were then stored in a little blue snap-close cover to hold them all together.

But security of the system was an issue. How was anyone going to know that the transactions being printed were legitimate transactions? Couldn't anyone with an IBM Selectric typewriter game the system, fraudulently printing out fake transactions at will and passing them off as actual updates from BMO? The solution, which I thought was superb, was that we would have a unique character that would appear only on the print ball of BMO terminals. Our little bar M would appear on anything that was printed from our system, and it could not be activated by anybody on the terminal at the branch level; only the centralized software controlled the bar M being printed at the end of the transaction. This little innovation to distributed banking sounds simple, but it represented a great security device thanks to centralized technology. The bar M symbol was unique to BMO and, therefore, we had to get IBM to manufacture custom print balls for us. The verification symbol printed at the end of any transaction meant that it was legitimate and done by the *Bank* — not by the individual teller. I thought it was ingenious.

The issues of the sort we faced at BMO in the 1970s and '80s around the economics and complexity of developing software solutions with business-wide applicability remain relevant today and are emblematic of the never-ending debate about centralization and decentralization in an organization. The complexity of today's organizations and the systems that run them — payroll and transportation scheduling systems being notorious among many others — force this question constantly. We have only to look at the monstrously costly disaster that is the federal government's Phoenix pay system to see the economic repercussions of not getting the balance right, and what happens when you don't make decisions about centralization vs. decentralization for the right reasons — as Austin Adams's comments at the beginning of this chapter so clearly point out.

TONY'S TAKEAWAY

Every leader is faced with the classic productivity riddle of centralization vs. decentralization and must understand and manage their push-pull dynamic for an optimal outcome in a complex, ever-shifting environment. While it's true that you can get more creativity from decentralized units, they can't always sustain themselves — when experiencing rapid growth, for example — and sometimes support is needed from centralized functions. Keeping the two forces in play is the key to robust productivity. The balance is what is important. And if my experience is any indication, the wheel will, I expect, forever turn.

VOICE: **HEATHER MUNROE-BLUM** OC

Heather Munroe-Blum is the retired principal and vice-chancellor of McGill University and has been a friend since I was an executive with the University of Toronto. We were also on the governing council together.

In 1995, the year after I began serving as a vice-president at the University of Toronto, I came across a situation where the books of a department did not balance. The possibility was raised that someone indirectly reporting to me was embezzling funds. Shocked, I sought the advice of the University's president while also immediately engaging an external auditor to initiate a complete audit of the department in question, myself and my office.

On the advice of the president, I also arranged a meeting with the chair of the university's board, Tony Comper, to disclose what was underway.

I was nervous, but with great kindness, Tony put me at ease, assuring me that in the world of business — or, for that matter, anywhere that a lot of money was in play — you had to be prepared for this kind of thing to arise. He encouraged me to pursue the truth relentlessly and without fear.

In the end, it turned out not to be a criminal problem, but a mental-health problem, and required not prosecution, but compassion — a quality that Tony so generously offered a young vice-president. From the moment I met him, Tony struck me as a deep and sincere thinker with a uniquely virtuous core. As he remains to this day.

CHAPTER 9

Listening Makes the World Go 'Round

The guilty think all talk is of themselves.
— GEOFFREY CHAUCER, *The Canterbury Tales*

I give Matt Barrett credit for the practice of our CEOs getting out to see the entire Bank operation, starting when we took over in 1990. He did the initial cross-country tour when we first took the reins, with him as CEO and me as president and chief operating officer. We laughingly called it The Matt Tour, and I joked about getting black satin windbreakers with "The Matt Tour" written in sequins on the back. (I could get away with saying that kind of thing to Matt; we had that kind of relationship.)

He went to eight or nine cities on his grand tour of the provinces to announce our agenda following Bill Mulholland's retirement. It was a great way to connect with employees and to hear their questions, concerns and feedback. Then Matt gave me his sardonic Irish smile and said, "Now, Tony, it's your turn." The expectation was that as COO, I would not just drop in on a handful of cities; I was to visit every single region in which we had operations. That might have been an even bigger deal in earlier times at the Bank when the organization was more far-flung and had more branches and regional offices. By the time Matt called on me, however, we had restructured the Bank, creating about 130 "communities" across the country, each with maybe six or eight branches. The plan was for me to spend three days getting to know the local business intimately. First, we'd bring everybody in the regional community to a local hotel on the morning of the first day, and I'd give a little bit of a town-hall talk. The next day I'd go to each of the branches in that immediate area and sit down in the lunchroom with the tellers and CSRs and lending officers and just let them talk about how they saw things at ground zero. On day three we'd concentrate on specific issues and problems we'd turned up in our earlier discussions. (The visits were also a good way to identify up-and-coming talent.)

The tour was extensive and exhausting, but it was also incredibly interesting and quite revealing. I'd find out all sorts of things I would never have discovered just managing the business from the sixty-eighth floor of First Canadian Place. In large organizations, not just a bank — media companies, manufacturers, government — there's a huge gap between the customer-service rep who knows what's wrong on the ground and the senior executives way up the line at headquarters in Toronto (or wherever) who have the capacity change it. There's no easy transmission of knowledge from the front lines to the executive level. Unfortunately, this is a common, chronic problem in all organizations, particularly in very large ones like BMO.

So how does a leader stay in touch with the business when you are located in downtown Toronto or Montreal or Vancouver — but your employees are spread out across the nation? The secret sauce is to have clear lines of communication, in both directions, and it starts at the top. Articulating clear objectives is the responsibility of every leader and manager throughout an organization. Only then can you put your vision and goals into action that produces the results you want. When that is achieved, the tricky part is putting processes in place to ensure that information is always flowing back to you from the front lines, that you are engaging with employees at all levels of the organization to close the crucial communications loop.

There's an interesting discussion about how corporations deal with this challenge in James Surowiecki's 2004 book, *The Wisdom of Crowds*. He shows how some companies believe that the dynamic of communication diminishes once you get to a certain number of employees. The theory is that no unit should have more than 150 employees. Rather than extend that number past 150, some companies will build a separate facility — sometimes just across the street — to accommodate more employees but in a separate unit that facilitates communication. In BMO's case, we handled this in part by dividing our operations across the country into 130 regions.

But even keeping your individual business units to 150 employees or fewer does not solve the problem entirely. There are several other reasons for a disconnect between workers and management. How do you cope with that pesky chain-of-command problem? It's absolutely essential to get the person or people who can make change out of the corner office to find out what's happening on the ground. That's what we did with our cross-country tours — which were *grinding*. For me, it was virtually two years of being on the road and going to places like Trail, British Columbia; or Elmira, Ontario; or Summerside, PEI. But the feedback was worth it.

The information we gleaned directly from our employees across Canada sometimes turned out to be the worst nightmare for the guy at Toronto head office who was running our retail branch system. I'd come in on Monday morning, fresh from the road, and say, "Time for our one-hour discussion." Then I'd give him a debrief on the fifteen things that I had picked up on my tour in the previous week. I can just imagine what he thought as I came through the door. For example, I was in the branch in Canmore, Alberta, talking to the staff. (We also have a branch nearby in Banff, but hardly anyone lives in the national park. Employees of the park almost all live in Canmore or Calgary.) A customer whose account was at the branch in Canmore had been in the park and was cashing a cheque in Banff. The Canmore people told me the Banff branch had called to get the transaction approved. And this was well after the introduction of any-branch banking!

I said, "Why is this happening when we are supposed to have any-branch banking?" As I mentioned earlier, I had personally programmed the software that enabled any-branch banking, which was supposed to stop us from making these sorts of phone calls to authorize funds. It was all supposed to be done online and via terminals. I was frustrated and maybe a little impatient when the Canmore staff brought up this issue.

"Yes, we know that, Mr. Comper, but the problem is the audit guys have told us that 'If you rely on the system alone and screw it up, you're the ones who are going to pay the penalty. You're going to have to swallow a loss if you get it wrong.'"

I assured them, "That won't happen, and the teller won't be found responsible for the loss because it . . ."

"Yes, but tell that to the audit guys."

Unbeknownst to us in head office, the same thing was happening in branches all across the country. We discovered that, notwithstanding the many millions that we'd put into software to make this sort of thing unnecessary, not all our divisions had gotten the message on any-branch banking. And we learned that the audit division was still requiring this process of phoning the branches for approval, which was time-consuming, unnecessary and not customer-friendly. That's not something we would have known about unless we had gotten out of the office. You wouldn't know. Nobody would know.

The retail division also had no idea until I brought them up to speed. I said, "You understand what's going on out there?"

They were was as mystified as I was as to why branches we're still phoning for approvals if we have any-branch banking.

"Aren't you guys supposed to know that?" This is why they dreaded the Monday-morning meeting with me.

It took twenty-four hours flat to change that policy. I called Marnie Kinsley, who was in charge of the audit department at the time. I said, "Marnie, guess what?" She didn't know this was happening either. The head of the audit department didn't know what her staff were doing out in the branches. We realized there was a profound disconnect between the two different business units of the Bank — retail and audit — that was having a real impact on our bottom line, counteracting the massive investment we had made in technology to improve productivity. And the only reason we discovered it as soon as we did was because I got out of the office and into the field to listen to the people who worked for us.

When these kinds of issues arose, I went back to some of my watchwords. First, I banked an awful lot on getting to know people and on not making snap judgments — I tried to think more analytically rather than only intuitively. Daniel Kahneman writes about these two different ways of processing the world in his book *Thinking, Fast and Slow*, calling them System 1 (intuitive, unconscious, emotional) and System 2 (analytical, conscious, calculating). Most of our lives, he says, we operate in System 1. People tend to answer difficult questions with intuition. But we simply can't analyze every single decision in life, or we'd go mad.

But sometimes these snap decisions will not suffice, and that's where System 2 comes in: making slower, more deliberative, and more logical decisions. That's how I tried to operate on these visits: the more I listened carefully to our staff, asked questions and probed for their concerns and feedback, the better judgment I was able to have as to their capabilities, their strengths and where they needed support.

The second maxim for me is articulating objectives. Employees are happier and more productive when they have a broader perspective on their role above and beyond the nine to five — a very clear view of what their objectives are supposed to be as well as the larger objectives of the organization. They feel a part of something bigger than their own job and that they are contributing. It's a great way of managing, and the question is, "Why don't most managers do this?" What happens if the boss is substandard and he doesn't know how to articulate what the objectives are, what he wants accomplished and why? Or what if the boss's boss did the same thing? It makes the whole chain break down. That's a lousy way to manage. If the bosses are incompetent in terms of articulating the objectives, then you can't hold the employees accountable nor can you fully engage them. It's all about getting results.

My third mantra is: Do the right thing. It sounds simple, but that's the test of every single problem, every single human issue. You think, what's the right thing to do? Faced with that question, I am sometimes reminded of a *Dilbert* cartoon. The workers are trying to solve a problem, and one of them says, "So what do we do now?" And the other one says, "Well what would Jesus do?" Okay, maybe that's a little glib. But it's another variation on "let's do the right thing," and it gives you a whole different view on how to solve a problem.

That cartoon has stuck with me. Maybe it's because in my early days I wanted to go into the priesthood (true on my part); my whole motive in life was, "What can I do to help others?" Later, I wanted to go to medical school to become a psychiatrist. I never made it, of course — I wound up being an English literature major. Then I ran a bank. But that desire to help others has stayed with me forever. When I was CEO of BMO, I believed that if we did the right thing, we'd wind up helping others one way or the other.

So what is the right thing? What is the right thing from an individual perspective, the right thing from a talent-management perspective, the right thing from a customer perspective? For a hypothetical example, just because our policies say that you should have advised us that you had lost your debit card and therefore it's your problem that you got ripped off for $300 — is it right to make customers pay in this circumstance? And are all our policies and cardholder agreements really clear or is our fine print like an insurance policy? Nobody ever looks at the mailer that goes out with your Mastercard, right? It's a bunch of legal gibberish getting the company off the hook in case you lose money. More often than not, credit card fraud isn't really the customer's fault; somebody simply ripped them off, and for us to hide behind the defence of, "It's right there in the small print . . ." isn't doing the right thing. In circumstances such as this, the company needs to use its judgment. Perhaps your response should be, like Dilbert: "What would Jesus do?"

Listening carefully to others to help resolve and support their needs is not just a bottom-up exercise. As much as we need to connect with our employees and customers to improve the way we are doing things, we also need to ensure that we are incorporating a number of different perspectives at all levels of the organization, particularly at the board level. The minute capitalism gets well established and developed, the concept of corporate governance becomes less of a passive thing and more of an active one. We rely on the varied leadership experience, critical analysis and sage counsel of our board to guide and govern how we do business. To get feedback from outside our comfort zone, we recruit directors according to a very explicit set of criteria and look for specific skillsets in terms of vetting potential directors for the Bank.

For example, so much of what we do in the Bank is governed by laws and regulations, and we need really strong leadership in this area. So, we have lawyers on the board who are highly skilled in these issues, people like Rob Prichard, who was the University of Toronto president but also a corporate lawyer. To build a diverse board, you also need people with varied backgrounds who are very plugged in to different aspects of the economy. In my day that meant people like Ralph Barford, who founded and ran General Steel Wares (GSW), a large company that manufactured appliances for GE and other businesses around the world. Or Bruce Mitchell, a small-business guy who had become wealthy developing five different companies and is highly sensitive to the needs and challenges of small- to medium-sized enterprises. There were many more like them.

Because so much of what the Bank does is governed by our political masters in Ottawa and various regulatory bodies, we were also careful to recruit directors with political savvy. Possibly the best example was Frank McKenna, a lawyer by training, and a very successful premier of New Brunswick. Because we had the Office of the Superintendent of Financial Institutions and others crawling all over us, forever doing inspections and audits, we needed the kind of political skillset that Frank McKenna brought to the table to help manage those critical relationships with governments and regulators. Ensuring that the organization is well-governed involves assembling a combination of very skilled people representing many different industries and disciplines, a wide range of business experience and the voices and perspectives of many different stakeholders.

I was, of course, on the board of directors from 1989 until my retirement in 2007. A lot of our time was spent on the big picture: vision, strategy, the direction of the business. Where is the Bank going in the future? What is the economy doing overall and how does that affect us? What about mergers and consolidations — where do they factor into the equation? Should we or shouldn't we be looking for partners? What's going on with the trend towards amalgamation in the U.S. market? Should we be expanding into the United States?

Over the years, I have been on many other boards in addition to BMO's, and in my experience, effective boards have a few key things in common. The directors — if they're really good — will be engaged, actively seeking to understand and get to the core of the major issues the organization is facing. They bring their own expertise and perspective to the table, helping to refine the key questions based on their experience. They will say, "Are you really sure? I mean, explain your thinking on that. Why do you think that's a good idea?" Effective board members are good communicators who are not afraid to challenge management's assumptions and decisions. When you're on a board, in many cases, you're also nurturing relationships with management and many other stakeholders to gain greater insight and leverage opportunities. Good directors do not simply show up, sit there and just take a cheque — they are actively involved in guiding the organization and ensuring that as many perspectives as possible are taken into consideration.

TONY'S TAKEAWAY

Like the visits I made to the regions to hear about local problems first-hand, there's a lot of essential, active listening that goes on at many other levels too. Clear objectives produce results that can change behaviour in individuals.

VOICE: **NANCY LOCKHART**

After a highly successful business career, Nancy continues as a valued board member of several diverse and significant companies. She has taken on leadership activities in theatre and community organizations. As she mentions, Liz and I met Nancy and her husband Murray Frum through our connection to the Stratford Festival. We became fast friends and continue to be so today after the passing of our spouses.

Despite Tony's conservative demeanour, he is possessed of a very robust and irreverent sense of humour.

I first met Tony and his wife Liz at the Stratford Festival where Tony and my late husband, Murray Frum, both served as board members. Not long after meeting, we arranged the first of many dinners together. Over the meal, I was introduced to his wide-ranging interests, his deep knowledge of history and his terrifically erudite and often amusing thoughts on matters of the day. I loved the fact that he was keen to poke fun at himself and to laugh uproariously while doing so. Liz, too, had a great sense of humour. Beneath that little-girl voice and "sugar wouldn't melt" persona was someone who loved to let the f-bombs fly to punctuate her views on this or that.

Tony has been extremely — but quietly — generous to many charities. He and Liz responded to an injustice they saw in society when they founded FAST, and together they supported hospitals, universities, the Art Gallery of Ontario and myriad other organizations. They provided funds but also many, many hours of hard work to support and shape the causes that were meaningful to them. In Liz's absence Tony has continued to grow his philanthropic reach and the initiatives he supports make a profound difference to the community.

Tony loves art and is an irrepressible collector with a great eye. His home is large, but the walls are becoming insufficient to hold all the wonderful paintings he has acquired. He is a particular supporter of women artists — an interest in line with his initiatives to support and promote women at the Bank. The broader public has been enriched by his gifts to the AGO, and he is always willing to lend to institutions so that as many people as possible can enjoy the paintings in his extensive collection.

Tony was a great husband to Liz, and they were inseparable until the day she died.

They were different in many ways but supported each other steadfastly — a great example of what marriage should look like.

I'm proud to call Tony my friend.

CHAPTER 10

Hidden Treasure:
Knowledge-Based Computing

For naturally a beast desires to flee
From any enemy that he may see,
Though never yet he's clapped on such his eye.
— GEOFFREY CHAUCER, *The Canterbury Tales*

I did some calculations — not recently, but some time ago. I worked out that in all the years I was working at the Bank — from 1961 until I retired in 2007, forty years of it full-time — I spent 37.5 percent of my time directly or indirectly involved with technology. So, I really spent less time as a banker than I did as a computer person.

I carried an old slide rule around for years and I'd show it to staff in the branches, young bankers, engineers and math students. By then it was a relic from days gone by, and several had no clue what it was or how to use it. I can do a calculation on a slide rule (or used to) faster than they could do it on a handheld computer. It was an unbelievably useful device and dead simple once you've got it. I didn't employ it a lot, but it did the job. I wasn't stubborn about it when the chance came to replace it. I used the money from my first bonus in 1975 to buy a Texas Instruments calculator that was programmable. It had little magnetic cards that you fed in the side, and you could program in information like algorithms and mathematical formulae. I found it very handy even as the technology changed at breakneck speed. Today, there is estimated to be many times more content on a microchip in your cell phone than we had in the huge early computers that filled a room.

The ease of interpreting data today is taken for granted. And it's all been made possible by the unexpected wonders of what we once called information technology, which I stumbled across in my software development days and which we now refer to as knowledge-based systems. I had been there when the IT revolution struck with all its power and glory in the 1970s. When technology arrived in full flight to change the very nature of banking, I was one of the first chief operating officers and later chief executive officers who was comfortable with computers. So, as an executive in the Bank, I had a unique appreciation for the capabilities as well as the challenges of our systems, and I could speak the software language well enough by the time people started approaching the Bank about investing heavily in tech in the early 2000s.

I had been there to sweat the details when you needed a large room in which to fit a computer. At one point, when I was in the technology group, the higher-ups decided to transfer me into the system-design department (which was responsible for defining the elements of a system such as the architecture, modules and components). One day, the manager of the department and the rest of the team were hyperfocused on some project that had nothing to do with me, so I thought it would be a great opportunity to figure out how to use the sort program. The sort program in the operating system had exits where you could take data out and manipulate the records in the process of them being sorted. Before they got through the sort and into the final configuration, you could modify them and then put them back into the sort process, all in real time.

I loved it. I was looking for a chance to try out some theories. My view was that, because we'd built a lot of transactional capability and operational functionality into our systems, we were starting to accumulate lots of information on our employees' habits and our clients' preferences that we hadn't necessarily anticipated we'd accumulate. I started to wonder, where does all that information go from here? What can it tell us?

Most people at the time would just say, "Sort these files," and it was our job in the system-design department to give them the information they'd requested and move on to the next task. But I was curious about the bigger picture and about what the information might tell us, so I wrote a sort exit to manipulate a certain class of records about teller functions. It took me about a week, but I loved it, because I learned so much about the internal configurations of the sort program and how it could be used in so many new ways. I began to realize the power of data to reveal patterns; the hidden treasure that lay in translating simple transactional information into insights that could support strategic initiatives and decision-making. As a senior manager and later an executive, I often used this thought process and our data to better understand our business and our customers, to move the Bank forward and to implement change. For instance, the same thinking process later enabled me to produce our research for our series of task forces on women, people with disabilities and Indigenous people, respectively. Decisions supported by information, facilitated by technology and based in evidence from the data have always suited my scientific, analytical mind. Nowadays, all managers take for granted the knowledge-based computing that helps them do their jobs, but back in my days in the system-design department, the process was still not very refined.

As important as it was to create software and use machines to assemble data back then, we were also challenged on how to organize that data in a workable form. Even when I became COO, we were still using a lot of what I called the old technology, such as print materials. How could we change the way we were doing things to use the growing amount of information at our fingertips in a more effective way? I thought, libraries are constantly acquiring and accumulating information, and they have experience in managing and accessing enormous amounts of knowledge. Maybe we could learn from them. So, when Carol Thomson, who had a Masters in Library Science, came on board at BMO to manage the library's compendia of printed information, we started collaborating on how to integrate the two technologies: the traditional print information and the capabilities of the new IT manipulation and storage technology.

The print technologies were moving towards more digitization and more storing of data online. But once you got it there, how could you use it to support the business? How could we access, use and interpret the huge volume of information our systems were constantly gathering? What was the role of IT in the process and how did that fit into supporting and informing management decision-making?

We had to think like computer programmers to understand what our systems were capable of (and I had the advantage there, thanks to all my years in the technology group), but we also had to think like librarians to understand how we could use the data we were capturing. The key was to start with the end goal of any business question, project or initiative and to work backwards to find the right information in the right format to inform our objectives and decisions.

We started working on articulating those goals very clearly and specifically to get at the information we would need to help achieve them. And then lo and behold, we hired Grant Reuber, who had built the economics department at the University of Western Ontario, eventually heading the department before becoming the first dean of the Faculty of Social Science and eventually chancellor of the university. In 1977, we hired him as BMO's chief economist. He left briefly in 1979 to become deputy minister of finance in the Joe Clark government and returned to the Bank when they lost power after only six months — this time in a much bigger job, as executive vice-president of the Bank's finance group. He also went on to serve as deputy chairman of BMO, president and chief operating officer. His was a brilliant mind and he had a distinguished career both in business and in academia.

Back when Grant was our chief economist, he called me up and said, "Tony, I've got this issue. When I look at the economics department, they've got these piles and piles of data, and when my guys are doing research they're clawing through all this printed material. Have you got a better way to automate all of these huge volumes of stuff that the economics guys pore through like crazy? It takes them forever to write a report." Grant could cut to the chase better than most; he knew exactly what he was looking for and for what purpose.

Carol and I immediately put our heads together to figure out how to get him what he needed. Carol and I put together a presentation to show Grant how decision support could play a meaningful role in integrating this kind of data into the business. I began, "Now, I'd like to introduce you to Carol, who's our librarian. She's going to do the presentation." Carol did a really good job, of course, and Grant recognized right away how some of the data the Bank was accumulating could improve the way information was used and interpreted in the economics department.

At the Bank of Montreal, and in every large organization today, we have this great storehouse of information that's been generated by our normal business activities that we can access quickly: who our customers are, what their buying or consumer preferences are, their demographic breakdowns and much more. It's a huge volume of data at our fingertips, a hidden treasure of personal information that we can use to achieve our business goals. But we also have a new proprietary responsibility to protect that data and to use it ethically.

In the age of Big Data, we are witnessing the power of information and of knowledge-based computing to an extent we have never seen before. Now we're seeing the role that accumulation of vast amounts of data has been playing in all businesses and in politics — and not necessarily the way I thought it would. It has segued to where the management of information is now extracting vast amounts of consumer data and using it in a way that was not the stated business purpose. The information that businesses and other organizations are gathering is too often crossing boundaries, being shared with other parties, compromising security and personal privacy and being used in ways that come into question in the U.S. Congress and Canada's Parliament. Companies are increasingly getting beaten up and reviled for misusing the very information they should be safeguarding. I've been watching these trends and developments with some interest.

Many technology-based companies have moved very quickly from where they started out to what they have become, and not everybody foresaw the implications or the downsides of their business model. Many social media companies, for example, very quickly moved away from simply being accumulators of data about their customers. In the process of such rapid growth and change, they didn't realize that they're not just in the distribution business; they had also become custodians of their customers' information. The responsibilities of a custodian are quite different than those of a distributor. Soon, people are asking you to pass editorial judgement on the material you've amassed.

Perhaps because we were involved very early with the creation of knowledge-based systems at the Bank, we've always understood that we are responsible custodians of our data, stewards of the vast amount of sensitive information we gather and keep about our customers. Of course, the regulators and the government wouldn't have it any other way, but we also recognize that this data is the hidden treasure that's at the core of our business. Naturally, we use the information we have to run our business, to sell and market more product to our customers and to make decisions that drive our profits and our success, but we guard it obsessively.

TONY'S TAKEAWAY

We've come a very long way from my early slide-rule days when I entered the Bank. Over my career I saw immense developments in technology and how it is integrated into the business. The greatest temptation with new technology is to believe it can do more than it is capable of. Find the line where human creativity intersects with algorithms: it's at the heart of our precious relationships with each and every customer who entrusts their financial life to us.

VOICE: CAROL THOMSON

Carol Thomson and I have known each other for almost four decades as friends, colleagues and collaborators. Early in our careers at BMO Carol, as head librarian, and I, as head of systems, worked on the integration of computer support for traditional economic research based on print materials. Carol went on to a highly successful business career including heading BMO Corporate Mastercard sales and American Express National Corporate Card Sales. More recently, Carol, with a graduate degree in library science, has assumed the role as curator of my unique and specialized library of rare books and first editions. She is a highly valued advisor, including suggesting the idea for the structure of this memoir.

I met Tony Comper in the fall of 1980 at the official opening of BMO's state-of-the-art computer centre in Scarborough, Ontario. He was the youngest VP in the Bank's history, and I was a newly hired librarian whose job it was to provide information services to systems staff. He was totally disarming and went out of his way to make a nervous new employee completely at ease. We found we had much in common. Tony had a keen interest in leveraging the resources of the Bank's business and technical libraries, which he felt were underused and underappreciated. To this end we worked on several initiatives to raise the profile of the libraries. We developed a long-lasting friendship.

Tony's impressive career accomplishments have been well documented. In his personal life, he has been instrumental in pioneering and supporting a wide range of causes — from advancements in medicine and human rights to the arts, education and many more. As the consummate problem-solver, he just can't resist trying to make situations better just because it's "the right thing to do," as he often puts it.

His non-denominational altruism sometimes baffled people. I remember a couple of years ago we were at a large gathering to celebrate one of Tony's friends, who was receiving an honorary PhD. Tony always attracted attention, and he was always being questioned about his philanthropic endeavours. FAST (Fighting Antisemitism Together) was one such initiative. At the party, a couple came up to say hello. While the husband asked about Tony's experience in disseminating student packages through the foundation, his companion had some questions for me.

"Did Tony have a Jewish background?" No.

"How about Elizabeth?" No.

"Was there a family connection or history associated with anti-Semitism?" No.

A thoughtful look came over the lady's face, and she said, "Well, I guess he's just a good man!" Yes. And I'm proud to call him a friend.

CHAPTER 11

Follow Your Rabbits

For he would rather have, by his bedside, twenty books,
bound in black or red, of Aristotle and his philosophy, than
rich robes or costly fiddles or gay harps.
— GEOFFREY CHAUCER, *The Canterbury Tales*

My old boss Bill Mulholland used to say, "Follow your rabbits." By that he meant, if your goals are important to you, pursue them wherever they go. For me, my rabbits at the Bank led me in the direction of investing in our workforce. How important is it for a corporation to invest in its people? To me, it's absolutely critical to sustainable success. I was the beneficiary of an excellent management development program very early in my banking career, and then was able to learn entirely new skills thanks to the Bank sending me to programmer's training school. I had to take a cut in pay to get in there, mind you — a dramatic cut in pay, and I had just gotten married. But developing a technology skillset opened up tremendous new opportunities for me and was ultimately my path to the C-suite. I have always been very grateful that the Bank was committed to my learning and development, and the crucial lessons about the value of training have stuck with me.

The Bank's traditional model had been learning on the job. You'd be trained by moving around from branch to branch and then moving into more progressive positions, learning from the others who had preceded you, gaining the skills that they, in turn, had learned from others who had gone before them. It was an apprenticeship system, basically.

Then, in the middle of the 1960s, the penny dropped for the Bank. As mentioned earlier, the Bank hired McKinsey & Company as consultants to get to the bottom of why they were losing competitive advantage. "We used to be the big dogs, but we aren't anymore. What happened?" Among other things, McKinsey said, "Well, structurally you've got some problems. But also, you've got an education problem. Increasingly, the best and the brightest young people are going to university, and you're not hiring university grads. You still believe in this learning-on-the-job model."

To their credit, the Bank bought the advice that McKinsey was selling. Our CEO at the time, Arnold Hart, started something called the President's Scholarship as one of his first initiatives to boost the Bank's commitment to education and development. This award was given to fifty young bankers who were top performers, allowing them to go to university while working. They were paid a full-time salary for four years while also getting a university education. Just before I took the HR job at head office and moved to Montreal in 1970, my boss at the time, Al Bates, had been one of those President's Scholarship candidates. He had won the gold medal in Commerce at McGill, tied with Gilles Jarry, another Bank of Montrealer who later got the gold medal and became another one of Hart's first recruits. Jarry went on to become senior vice-president of BMO's Quebec division.

The positive results from that first cohort of fifty candidates, even in the early days of the program, got the Bank thinking about the importance of education. So, in 1967, the Bank started what was called the special development program. That was the one I had been hired into, where university graduates could become a branch manager within five years.

In 1970, the year I went to Montreal to work, they started yet another program called the Youth Project, managed by Ivan Eaton, who had been the head of the YMCA in Toronto. Again, it was the brainchild of Arnold Hart, intended to give lower-income kids career opportunities. The program targeted young kids with potential who may not even have had the chance to make it through high school. It could have been someone who had a job supporting a spouse and three kids but not much formal education. The idea was to take them into the program and give them remedial education for six months in the basic skills of banking and business. Plus, the Bank would guarantee them a job and pay them a salary if they stuck it out to the end. But it was tough love — if you slacked off for one minute or didn't show up, you were out.

And it worked. In fact, a couple of those kids were still working in senior management positions at the Bank when I was there. After the Bank of Montreal program had been running for several years, other major Montreal companies — Bell, CN, Redpath Sugar — got on board, too. I don't know if the program still exists, but it turned into a consortium of large corporations helping lower-income kids who hadn't had a chance to complete their education, for whatever reasons.

On the heels of the McKinsey engagement in the mid-1960s, the Bank decided that it needed to bring in some fresh blood to beef up the training and development function in the HR department. Fred McNeil had been a newspaper guy out in Calgary, then wound up in management at the Ford Motor Company before being recruited by the Bank. I had a lot of time for Fred, and we got on quite well, even though I was just a kid at the time. He knew that we were deficient in a couple of areas, so he hired a bunch of other Ford Motor Company colleagues and they became the human resources guys.

One of them was Bob MacDougall, who had a master's degree in statistics, and he had been a university professor as well. When Bob came on board, he pushed the Bank's technology, and therefore its training needs, in a whole new direction. He was the one who wrote the proposal for a revolutionary kind of computer system that would automate transactional processes, gather unprecedented amounts of data and that would be the harbinger of any-branch banking, which none of the other banks were doing. It was to be called the Online Banking Project. It certainly was revolutionary at the time and he realized that to make it all work, we needed computer people who understood banking rather than having bankers and software people in completely separate orbits. That's when they began to run a recruitment program across the Bank for young people with banking knowledge who also were interested in being trained in computer technology.

As you know from earlier chapters, I started out recruiting those people and then I became one of them. I was so intrigued by the work they were doing, I asked if I could get into the program too. It was heady stuff, and to me it seemed like the coming wave. I wasn't really thinking about the future or economics or anything else for myself; I was simply excited about learning all about computer technology.

Well, you know the story of what happened from there: I advanced through the computer group, eventually becoming vice-president of systems. I kept the programmer training school as a critical staff intake point. I don't know the exact number, but I think we put somewhere between three hundred and five hundred young people through this program when I was running the system.

We had the lowest turnover rate of anybody in the computer industry, and I was proud of that. Why was ours so low? Because, in each class we had a cadre of twelve kids with a common interest. They'd spend six months in school together, and they would bond as friends. They'd go onto the floor and become computer programmers and professionals, but they always had their friendship and their class of 1975 or whatever year. And they stayed.

Some of them would go elsewhere, of course, because they were hot properties. But many would come back after a few years because they wanted to be with their friends. It was technology and it was work, but it was also a supportive social environment. We had a 5 percent turnover rate in an industry that averaged about 35 percent, and that translated into an incredible return on our investment in training and a considerable economic contribution to the Bank's bottom line. Turnover is a very expensive factor: training employees to meet your expectations is a two-way street. Give as good as you get with their intellectual property — invest in the education and training of your staff and they will pay you back many times over.

By 1990, Matt Barrett and I had moved into the most senior positions in the Bank, with Matt at the helm. He was always intrigued with the power of formal education. His dad had been a bandleader in Ireland, and then Matt, like a lot of young Irish guys, went off to London, England, to make a life for himself. He joined Bank of Montreal in England as a junior clerk. Always a smart guy, he worked his way up. He came to Canada because we were recruiting from the

U.K. back in the 1970s. It was Britain pre–Margaret Thatcher, and the country was in a mess economically. People were anxious to get out, so we were recruiting like crazy for bankers from the U.K. And Matt came to Canada as part of that influx.

As I said, Matt was always a great believer in education — even if he didn't have a lot of postsecondary schooling. As a result, one of the earliest things he did was create what's now the BMO Institute for Learning (IFL). Originally they wanted to call it the Learning Centre but I suggested it should have a more professional, university-type designation. Matt said we couldn't call it a university, but we could call it an institute, which has a European kind of cachet to it. And so it became the Bank of Montreal Institute for Learning.

But this was also happening in the throes of the 1990 financial downturn, so I said, "Matt, you're being stubborn as hell. There were other great needs throughout the Bank when we took over." There had been a lot of underinvestment in the branch system, and they were screaming for more first-line customer service people. We had a list of branches that we called the Dirty Thirty — branches that had not had a repair done to them for decades. They were falling down and the Bank had underinvested in these physical assets. So was this a good time to spend $50 million on some institute that was going to have a payback far in the future rather than investing in today's needs? "Why aren't we hiring more tellers?" I asked Matt.

The shame on me was, having gone through programmer training school and understanding the Bank's commitment to pay for me to go to school for six months on full salary — even reduced or frozen salary — I should have known better. Education and continuous learning were fundamentally important to the success of the organization. And even though I pushed back at Matt for investing in the Institute for Learning when he did, I understood the value of it. My point was, the timing was not good, and the economics were sketchy. I said, "Our shareholders are going to be looking to kill us for putting $50 million into this Taj Mahal of a learning facility. They're going to hate us." I would say to him, "You've got a completely legitimate argument, but you know what? There's only so much money to go around, and we can't spend ourselves into oblivion in the short run because otherwise the whole place is going to go to hell in a handcart. And the staff want us to put money into upgrading the branches."

Matt just looked at me. "Tony, thank you for your input. But no."

Stubborn Irishman, right? (People say I'm stubborn, but you should have seen Matt when his mind was made up.) Guess what? I was dead wrong about it; Matt was absolutely right. Instantly, the staff went into it saying, "I'm very proud that the organization I work for has the foresight to invest in my learning and my development." The interesting thing is, instinctively, the people who worked for the Bank understood everything we did. They knew we were investing in them as much as we were investing in the future of the Bank.

The Bank of Montreal Institute for Learning was like all of Matt's best ideas: he would announce them and then hand them to me. I had to be the engineer, working out the details to accomplish his vision. On the Institute, I was working with Raymond Moriyama, the famed architect. I suggested that if we were going to do it, we had to add live-in facilities. I suggested we design the school to be more like a classical college in the U.K., à la Cambridge, with a quadrangle and living accommodations — and that's what we did. The BMO IFL is located in Scarborough on the east side of Toronto. The place is beautiful, a jewel in the crown of our commitment to education and learning. The business end, the training facility, classrooms, meeting rooms and so on are on one side of the building, and then it wraps around a classic college quadrangle with single rooms and a gymnasium.

I was surprised by the reaction of the staff to it — I was amazed, actually. I would go up there all the time, and I'd meet, for example, a woman in a senior managerial position in Saskatchewan on a one-week or two-week program. She had never been to Toronto, so she'd brought her daughter with her. In addition to the training programs she was also enjoying the cultural experience of the city. It was a double benefit, and she really appreciated it.

The next thing was Ron Rogers, my executive vice-president for domestic banking, saying to me, "We've got a lot of young people working for us who've got an undergraduate degree in commerce or something else, but they don't have an MBA. They've got a family and kids and they can't take time off to go back to school. Can we develop a program whereby they can get an MBA while working full-time on the job? Tony, what do you think?"

I had good connections with the University of Toronto, and I told Ron I'd talk to the business school there. Tiff Macklem, now governor for the Bank of Canada and formerly dean of U of T's Rotman School of Management, took me out to lunch, and I told him the story of how the U of T administration at the time reacted. "They said, 'Oh Tony, you don't really understand education and learning. You can't have an MBA program that's exclusive for your own employees. You have to have the benefits of people from other companies joining our executive program,' which was, I believe, quite expensive."

Now that U of T was off the table, I turned to Dalhousie. I explained the program once again — they could design the program for Bank of Montreal employees to continue working while Dalhousie professors would teach them at the Institute of Learning, allowing them to earn a Dalhousie MBA in Finance. Unlike U of T, Dalhousie jumped at the chance.

We've now put hundreds of people through this excellent program.

Although Bank of Montreal was the oldest bank in Canada and our corporate headquarters had been in Toronto since 1977, we were still regarded as "the Montreal guys," *nouveau* on Bay Street. We were the *arrivistes* coming to Toronto. I said to Matt, "Now we've got to change our profile. We've got to get involved in high-profile community activities. You're going to try to get on the board of the Toronto General Hospital, and I'm going to try to get on the board of the University of Toronto." Which is exactly what we eventually did.

I went on to have a long-lasting association with U of T. I became chair of the governing council, then we launched the capital campaign in 1997. I also became chair of that major fundraising campaign, and the expectation was the Bank would be a big contributor — they came through with a million dollars. The overall campaign goal was for a billion dollars, and we hit it. It was the biggest private-sector fundraising campaign in the history of Canada.

The Bank turned its generous donation of a million dollars into an opportunity to support the university in a specific and tangible way. At that time the University of Toronto had something called the National Scholarship Program, which they developed to counteract the brain drain of many of Canada's smartest kids being lured to top U.S. universities on a full scholarship. And they were not only smart academically, they were also school leaders who played sports and participated in all sorts of activities and causes.

These most promising kids simply couldn't afford to go to the University of Toronto when they were being given a full scholarship elsewhere. So the university created the National Scholarship Program to pay students accepted into it for their tuition, as well as their room and board, and make it economically viable for them to come. At BMO, we wanted to effectively sponsor that program to promote Canadian university education, using a chunk of our million-dollar donation to support it. The program runs to this day, still supported in part by BMO. I don't know how many there are in the cohort. Every year we have a dinner at the Bank — not just for the current crop of kids but for all the alumni who are now doctors, scientists and other accomplished professionals across Canada and around the world.

One last story about the Bank and education: because we were around before all the other banks, we became the banker to virtually all the universities in the country in the early days. Look at the Maritime schools or McGill or any of them: we were the banker for all of them. We'd put Bank of Montreal branches on the campuses of all the schools, which proved to be a smart strategy. That may have changed in recent years, but if you went to the University of New Brunswick or the University of British Columbia or to Western, you'd see a Bank of Montreal branch or at least a few ABMs. Students got used to dealing with the Bank of Montreal. It wasn't necessarily a moneymaker in the short run, but it sure was a great program for building customer loyalty early.

Frank McKenna, the former premier of New Brunswick and former BMO board member, will to this day say that one of the best people that he's ever known was the Bank of Montreal branch manager at the University of New Brunswick, where he went to law school. We had a campus branch there and the manager was a really smart woman, one of our first female branch managers in the country. Frank said all he had to do was to go in and talk to her and she would help manage his finances. She was terrific. And people like her created customers for life. I couldn't be prouder when I see graduates from our various education programs at annual banquets or when they simply come up to me on the street and thank BMO for the opportunity they had.

TONY'S TAKEAWAY

Training and education are among the best investments you can make, in a business and more broadly in society. Give as good as you get with your talent. Training employees will not only enable them to meet your organizational goals; you will be rewarded with loyalty and their larger contribution to your business. Education is a two-way street. We at BMO can count the return in the thousands of employees and scholars we've touched over the years.

VOICE: JACK O'BRIEN, PART 2

I remember once when Tony was working at the Bank of Montreal while I was teaching high school in north Toronto. It was a Thursday, and we'd agreed to meet at the Bay Bloor Tavern for beer at eight o'clock in anticipation of the weekend. It wasn't a great time for Tony, because he was just getting out of work and hadn't eaten much — nor for me, because a few beers on a school night makes for a long next day of teaching. That said, I was at the bar early and was well into my third beer when Tony arrived.

"Doesn't the bank close at three?" I asked, because, by now, it was closer to nine than eight. "What the heck can you have been doing all this time?"

I'd obviously managed to keep the irritation out of my voice, because without missing a beat Tony started explaining how the Bank needed to keep records of every transaction for five years, and they'd been piling up helter-skelter in the basement of the branch he was assigned to at that time. On this day, as almost every day since he'd started at the branch, he'd been down there since the bank closed putting those records in chronological order.

"Anyone else stay?" I asked.

"No, the last of them left at five or six."

"But there must be a billion of those transaction records," I said, incredulous. "How long do you think it will take you to finish?"

"Probably never," he replied. "But you've got to start somewhere."

Maybe *you* do, I thought. But sure as hell not me.

This stays with me because I just can't believe that someone as smart as Tony would undertake and stick to such a boring, thankless and

— to my mind — useless task. It's only years later when computers and spreadsheets and databases are everyday items that I realize how a guy with Tony's mindset would take to them like a duck to water and how that would make him a natural for advancement in modern banking.

CHAPTER 12

Tapping into All Our Talent: Women and Diversity in the Bank

Her hand a bow with arrows cased and keen;
Her eyes were lowered, gazing as she rode
Down to where Pluto has his dark abode.
— GEOFFREY CHAUCER, *The Canterbury Tales*

Joyce Acton was the first of many formidable and talented women I worked with at the Bank over my forty-year career. It was 1969, I was in the credit-officer training program, and Joyce was my boss. That was unusual at the time; women simply weren't considered management material. Joyce broke the mould and was one of the first women to start chipping away at the Bank's very thick glass ceiling.

The story went that she was the daughter of the cop-on-the-beat at the King and Yonge branch, and her father had gone to the branch manager, telling him about his very smart daughter and asking if he could give her a job. The branch manager, impressed by what the officer had told him, thought it over and ended up hiring Joyce as his secretary. It quickly became obvious to everyone that Joyce was indeed really smart and shouldn't be stuck in a lowly administrative position. Don Munford, an assistant manager in the branch at the time — he ultimately became the head of our credit department and a very close friend of mine — spied her and said, "She's smarter than that." He broke all the rules to get Joyce absorbed into the management stream. And eventually she went on to glory as a senior credit person at BMO. There were other pioneers, too, like Rebecca Watson, who became the first female branch manager in 1963 when she took over a branch at the University of New Brunswick.

In my early days at the Bank, these kinds of success stories about women's careers were rare, but I encountered another strong, accomplished woman in a position of influence when I moved to head office in Montreal in 1970. Maureen Maguire held a senior position in the technology department at the time I moved over into that group from HR. She was Irish and very tall, and had a wonderful sense of humour. I was still single at the time, so Maureen, her friend Heather, Heather's boyfriend and I would hang out together. She'd say, "Come on, Comper, we're going out for a martini at 7:37 [the name of the bar at the top of Place Ville Marie]. You know, their martinis are really great. They're so dry you have to pee in a sandbox." And laugh? Could she laugh.

Maureen was my boss too. She ran the Bank's whole computer-application department at the time. That was before I went into programmer training school. She was so good at her job — she was brilliant and such a great manager. I was lucky to have worked so closely with two such influential women so early in my career. And that started me thinking. I saw very quickly that they were the equal of any man and that there was the potential to tap into far more female talent, both in the banking system and in the technology group — indeed throughout the enterprise and at every level.

I have always been a strong proponent of equal opportunity for women in the workplace, and I'm proud to say that I started several initiatives at BMO to support the advancement of women in their careers and into leadership roles. My mantra always has been, "It's not just a smart thing to do for our business; it's also the right thing to do, for women and for society." The argument for removing artificial blockages to advancement of women in our Bank was, for me, foremost an economic issue — it's good for our shareholders, but it's also a good thing to do. So when we came to address the issue of women in the upper ranks of the Bank, it was not just a do-good argument. That was a major part of it, of course, but the argument was also an economic one. Not tapping into the potential of the talented women in our company meant that we were underleveraging a tremendous economic resource.

That's a huge disservice to the shareholders as well as to the women who were being held back.

In the 1970s when I started working at the Bank full-time, unconscious systemic discrimination was still keeping women out of the executive ranks; they were restricted to the lower levels of the organization without much appreciation for their talents, potential or opportunities for advancement. What a waste. I started thinking about the issue then and when I became a recruitment coordinator in the computer department at head office, I knew we had to do something different. The whole technology area was brand new at the Bank and growing very quickly. Hardly anyone had the qualifications and experience we were looking for, but we needed to fill positions quickly; we didn't have the luxury of being picky in the hiring process. We used to joke that all you needed to be hired were two things: one, you had to be able to program; and two, you had to be able to fog a mirror. If those two criteria were met, then you were in.

Okay, I exaggerate. But we needed all the talent we could get.

As a new vice-president in 1978 at age thirty-two, I had already seen the light: talent meant everything, and gender meant nothing when it came to talent. My observation then was that this was going to change the Bank. The staff in the computer programming department was almost a 50/50 split between men and women. This ratio existed nowhere else in the Bank, but the technology department represented the cutting edge of where things were going. I was certain that was the way it would be in the rest of the Bank too. But then I also quickly realized that although women were well represented as programmers, all the department managers were men, even in the technology department, which I had thought was so progressive. I wondered, "Hmm. What's going on here?"

Now, fast forward to when Matt Barrett and I were handed the reins of the Bank. I said, "You know, Matt, this has been bugging me for a long time. When you look at our workforce, it's primarily women." There was, in part, an economic reason for that, by the way. Up until the Second World War, most of our employees had been men. Then they all went off to war, so the Bank hired women to fill the vacant spots. Even after the war, the women stayed on in those positions, quickly transforming our workforce. (Contrary to my *festina lente* philosophy that things don't change quickly, when you're really forced to do something, change can happen fast.) "But," I also pointed out to him, "Women are hardly anywhere to be seen at the management level."

Then I bolstered my argument by digging into the numbers I had produced from our computer data mining, quantifying it for Matt. "This is really ridiculous," I said. "When you look at our total work-force, 74 percent of our employees are women. Then look at the executive level: only 6 percent are women." In my view, that was an unaccept-able imbalance. My thesis was that we were underleveraging what was a significantly powerful economic resource and perpetuating a funda-mental lack of fairness in our organizational values.

To even begin to create a more equitable workplace, we first had to defeat several deeply ingrained stereotypes. First, the conventional wisdom that women join the Bank for a short period of time, then quit to have kids. Second, that women's tenure in the Bank is dramatically lower than men's. Three, their education levels are dramatically lower than that of men. The generally accepted thinking was that men were university-educated and pursued careers, whereas the women came straight out of high school and worked part-time. And added to that was the belief that their performance levels were probably not at the same level as men. All of these ideas involved a lot of sweeping assumptions and, as a fan of the scientific method, I was determined to prove them wrong. So I said, "Guess what, Matt? We've got a very sophisticated computer database. And it's got all the data on whether that's true or not."

In the meantime, we found ourselves on stage at Roy Thomson Hall in 1990, introducing ourselves after we'd begun taking command at Bank of Montreal. Matt was sitting onstage on a stool doing his best standup routine — a combination of wit, candour and irreverence. Matt loved a good Q & A segment. He'd get one question, and then he would give a twenty-seven-minute answer. This was Matt at his finest; he was always very good at this sort of extemporizing — far better than I will ever be in a million years.

Then a woman in the audience put up her hand and said, "Mr. Barrett, when you look at this huge room here, it's all women. Most of the Bank's employees are women. But when I look at the top of the

Bank, it's all men. Can you explain that?" Matt did a John Cleese pause, and he replied, "You know what? That's an excellent question. And I'm glad you asked it, because I'm very pleased to announce Mr. Comper has just started a task force on the advancement of women in the Bank." Standing ovation.

And I'm sitting there thinking, "What?" You see, Matt had listened to me even though I thought I wasn't getting through to him. He'd picked up on the point that I had made to him, and in his mind he knew that he could turn that into this opportunity. And when I heard him announce my name I thought, "Holy . . . " because I'm always good at having the ideas and floating them, but I'm not as good at being brave enough to actually take the initiative, get my ass in gear to get out there and do it.

That staff gathering in Roy Thomson Hall started the whole Employee Task Force on the Advancement of Women in the Bank, which would take on a life of its own, inspire other task forces and effect positive change throughout the organization. But for it to be accepted and to work, I needed it to be done with a scientific method; it couldn't be just anecdotal. I started very carefully by picking the right people to be on the taskforce, including Ron Call, Deanna Rosenswig, Penny Somerville, Harriet Stairs, Rob Tetley and Jane Weatherbie.

Then we could begin the process of assembling empirical information from our computer database to help make the case for what we wanted to accomplish. And sure enough — "Research says!" — as I had suspected, women's tenure at the Bank was equal to, or better than, men's, with sixteen to seventeen years on average. Their education level was equivalent to men: just as many female employees had undergraduate degrees as men, and many also had MBAs and other graduate degrees. Performance levels were equal to or better than men. Anything else you wanted to learn about, guys?

And so began the Task Force on the Advancement of Women in the Bank. We pored over all this data and much more, working to overturn a bunch of false assumptions about women in the workforce and to break down the barriers to their success. Our research culminated in a detailed report that we published in 1991. Among other things, it concluded that the discrimination against women in our culture was endemic. It wasn't a deliberate, conscious kind of thing; it was just the way it had been for many, many years. Self-perpetuating. That may seem so obvious today, but it was pretty advanced thinking at the time and, more importantly, it was backed up by strong empirical evidence. We had the numbers to prove what we had suspected for years — and now, we had the power to change it.

I distributed the report not just to our employees but had it published for general consumption. I made a point of spreading the word about what we were doing with the Task Force on the Advancement of Women in the Bank. I felt very strongly that we should make it public, because it could benefit women, organizations and society in general throughout Canada. The only way we were really going to tackle this issue permanently was if we got the research out broadly to get people talking and making some real change based on facts. Naturally, there was an outcry from people in the Bank who didn't want to give the competition any advantage, but my philosophy was that we were so far ahead of the pack it wouldn't matter if we released all the information. It had taken us four long years to get to this point, and even if our competition took all the findings to heart, they wouldn't be able to catch up to us anytime soon. So we made the report public in 1994.

Endemic discrimination is not necessarily intentionally malicious, or even conscious. People will naturally hire people who are like them. And so men in senior positions will hire other men in senior positions to work for them — that's just a fact of human nature. But the net effect is still the same: inequity, injustice and serious economic consequences, both for the affected individuals and for organizations and society at large. To fix all that is a complicated issue.

As we embarked on the process of change, we had to walk a very fine line, because the inevitable instant reaction you're going to get nailed with, particularly when using data and numbers to guide the initiative, is, "Ah, you're going have a quota system?" My standard response was, "No, because we're never going to give up on merit as the principal criterion for who gets hired and promoted. As it turns out, if you cast the net wide enough to include women, you will find even more people who have the skills we're looking for."

To sensitize our managers and employees to the issues, I started men-and-women-as-colleagues sessions. We began at the leadership level with a group of three or four senior women and a group of three or four senior executive men, and they'd talk about the issues — concerns, barriers, policies, specific examples of gender discrimination and how to overcome it. It was generally very uncomfortable for bankers to get outside their wheelhouse and into a touchy-feely subject like gender disparity. But we had to bring the problems to the surface in order to fix them. Next, we moved the sessions to the general population of the Bank.

Making change was a slow, sometimes painful, process and just when I thought the task force was making progress, I would talk with someone and it would feel like we'd taken several steps back. I remember a conversation with one of our managers, who was shocked by the data results, and realized we were on to something. "We've got to fix that, Tony," he said. Then he added, "Thank God it doesn't happen in my department." And, of course, his department was one of the worst for gender discrimination statistically. He was eager to fix the problem but wouldn't admit it was his problem too.

I countered resistance by telling our managers, "You've got to give everyone an equal chance. So whenever you come to me with a recommendation for a promotion to a senior job, I want to see who the women candidates for that job are. These need to be legitimate candidates with the same skill levels as the men. Put those candidates down on a sheet of paper." The idea was that forcing managers to go through the process of actively considering female candidates would start to have an impact.

And women weren't just being shut out of jobs in the C-suite, the executive ranks and promotions to management in those days — it went much deeper than that. Perhaps this scenario will give you some idea of what we were up against. It's a specific example but it happened more often than you might think. There'd be a luncheon for a couple of clients, and I'd have a look at who was going to attend the meeting. I'd say, "But isn't Diane Lapaix the account manager for this particular customer?"

"Uh, yeah."

"So why isn't she invited to the lunch?"

"Well, she's an account manager."

"Yes, and that's why she should be there. Don't the clients know she's the account manager?"

"Yeah."

"Aren't they going to be surprised that she isn't at the lunch?"

That sort of eye-opening conversation took about three-and-a-half seconds to get around the Bank: "You'd better watch it. Comper's on the warpath." Soon, female account managers started showing up at client luncheons all over the place.

And word got out to the larger community what we were doing. There's a global non-profit organization called Catalyst, founded in New York by Felice Schwartz back in 1962, and dedicated to the advancement of women in business. Every year, Catalyst presents an award to a company doing meaningful things towards the advancement of women. There is stiff competition, and their due diligence process can take six to eight months, at the end of which they present the award at an annual conference and awards dinner. BMO received the prestigious Catalyst Award in 1994, the first bank in North America to do so; in fact, it was the first Canadian organization of *any* description to do so.

We had done some very important work and Catalyst had recognized us for it. Then an amazing thing started to happen. Women at all levels in other banks went in to see their bosses, telling them, "If you don't start doing something the way BMO has done, we're out of here." So instantly the other banks got the religion, which is a wonderful thing.

TONY'S TAKEAWAY

The focus on the advancement of women in the Bank is one of the things that I am proudest of in all of my career. It was not only a good thing to do, but it was important for the shareholders. In a competitive industry like financial services, all of us must strive for all the edge we can get. For us at the Bank, that meant empowering the women we had in our company. The rest is history.

VOICE: DIANE FRANCIS

Diane Francis is an extremely successful journalist and polit-ical commentator. Our collaboration, described by Diane, focused on an initiative to recognize successful women entre-preneurs. Diane was fond of recounting to me the support she received from BMO on her immigration to Canada in the 1970s. I was very lucky to have her husband, John Beck, join the board of the Crown Corporation I chaired.

In 1992, I started the Canadian Women Entrepreneur Awards with Mona Bandeen. She was head of Women's Studies at the University of Toronto, and she approached me — after I became the first female editor of a daily newspaper — to launch awards to celebrate women in business. We enlisted several sponsors, including the Bank of Montreal, who supported the awards program in a big way for many years. When they decided to come on board, we invited Tony and Liz to the gala dinner. Tony would hand out several of the awards that evening.

In our third year, our awards evening conflicted with the men's big award, CEO of the Year, but Tony decided to attend the Canadian Women Entrepreneur of the Year event that night instead of appearing at the CEO award. I thought, "Wow. That was so cool." I was emcee, as usual, and mentioned that he had chosen to be at our celebration over the men's, and he got a standing ovation.

To me, his decision revealed something very unique about Tony (I'm sure it was partly Liz's influence): he was a feminist at heart. He was one of the few in the business establishment who would have made the choice he did. It was really quite stunning and impressive to me.

About that time, BMO started to roll out a number of very important initiatives that helped a lot of women get into the business world and get loans. Tony was a pioneer in establishing and supporting those programs. He was attuned to an issue that few other CEOs in Canada even recognized. As I've often said, a country that denies education and opportunities to women is denying half the IQ of the country. You've thrown away half the talent. Tony was the first leader of a major corporation to say, "Yeah, I agree, and I'm going to implement strategies to change that." Every time I saw him after that and there were other people around, I would make a point of saying, "This is the guy and this is what he did." I just thought it was really stand-up first class.

CHAPTER 13

Riding the Tiger of Corporate Citizenship

If you are poor your very brother hates you
And all your friends avoid you, sad to say.
— GEOFFREY CHAUCER, *The Canterbury Tales*

Today, in the information age, corporations are under closer scrutiny than ever before for their policies and actions. Not only are we accountable to our shareholders, but more and more we are also answerable to the general public, who increasingly call the corporate sector on the carpet for everything from inappropriate management behaviour to fuelling the climate crisis.

Corporate accountability has had many different labels over the years — including corporate social responsibility or just good corporate citizenship — and a more socially aware culture can now use social media to quickly amplify their opinions. The fact is people want to do business with companies they admire and respect. So why should people bank with, or work at, or invest in BMO? What makes BMO so special? What are we doing to be good corporate citizens, to be responsible stewards of the financial assets our customers entrust to us, and to stay attuned to the priorities of our stakeholders and the public in general?

I'm a little biased, and although the definition of what it has meant to be a good corporate citizen has evolved over the years, I like to believe BMO people and BMO thinking have always been on the crest of the public wave.

One moment in particular reinforces for me our place in the community — and my own commitment to that standard. Back in 1990, I was fairly new to the job of chief operating officer, and Matt Barrett was in his early days as CEO. It was around the time of the real-estate downturn in the economy. Not easy days. But we felt it was important to keep an annual tradition alive for our staff. For several years, we had been booking Canada's Wonderland for a day in May to offer our staff a fun outing. It would be before the park was officially open for the season — a soft opening just for us. We got inexpensive tickets for all of our staff and not only were the employees welcome, but their kids and their cousins and their uncles and their aunts and so forth were also invited.

I remember being up on the Kingswood Theatre stage at Wonderland and looking out to the 15,000 or 20,000 people in attendance, people looking up at us as we prepared to say a few words. I could just feel the sense of responsibility. All these people were dependent for their livelihood on us getting things right in a tight economic time. I said to Matt, "Do you realize what the responsibility is here? It's not just us; it's not just the employees. There's a whole community of people who are associated with us in one way or another who are dependent on us being successful." I could feel it, the responsibility. That's what I mean by corporate accountability.

Standing there in front of the crowd took me back to when we were trying to get the software working for the online banking system in the 1970s. It seemed we might never get it right. But we had to. That's another form of accountability. In the technology department in those days, we all felt the responsibility to get it right for the organization, our customers, our shareholders. And that translated to an incredible personal ownership that we all felt over the role we played and the job we had to do.

The higher I went up the ranks at the Bank and the bigger my job got, the more I felt that sense of responsibility. And as a leader, you can't be afraid to adapt your attitude to changing times and changing circumstances. For instance, in my retirement speech in 2007, I said that corporate accountability meant "our industry's doing what our industry can to prevent the environment from being despoiled and people from being abused by future generations of global mega-projects. We are making our funding contingent upon our environmental sustainability."

What did I mean by that? That we not be tied to companies and issues like — I don't like the term but I'll use it anyhow — the blood-diamond trade and other such rapacious, exploitive practices. That we take care to be environmentally sensitive, filtering our investments through that lens. Part of the point I was trying to make was that in this day and age, only at your own peril would you fight the fight against the environment.

Corporations have a role in effecting positive change, not only for their own business results, but also for their stakeholders and the broader communities in which we live, work and invest. And in my tenure as a senior manager at BMO, I have seen the call for corporate account-ability manifest itself in many ways, focused on causes that every socially aware person would agree upon. For example, the rampant clear-cutting of the old growth forest in British Columbia received a great deal of publicity for a while from environmentalists. They were saying that there are better and more sustainable logging practices, and now the smart forest management companies are harvesting much more responsibly.

Let's pick another classic example: apartheid in South Africa. The investment community was still investing there into the 1980s. I don't care who you are — what was going on there was not right. I remember at a Bank meeting that some spectators were reading a speech that Nelson Mandela had made when he was in jail, proclaiming that he just might get himself killed for making this very speech. When the nuns started to come to BMO's annual meetings to demand that we stop supporting the apartheid regime by lending them money, that's when we knew we had to divest from South Africa. Their government was flagrantly flying in the face of any kind of decency or human rights and we, and others, were made to see that we would be complicit in their violation of those rights if we continued to do business in that country.

Our CEO at that time, Bill Mulholland, understood that there is a need for caution when dealing with bad actors, an aspect to which you've got to be sensitive. So we wouldn't finance arms dealers, for example. Mulholland simply refused to do so, saying, "We won't finance arms dealing because we believe it's wrong." Same with the environment.

Even the climate-change skeptics would agree that the flagrant violators were doing harm to the natural world.

One of my favourite examples of corporations being called out for their lack of environmental stewardship — and being made to change their ways to improve the situation — is the acid-rain issue in the 1970s and '80s. There was conclusive evidence that emissions from coal- and oil-fired power plants, smelters, motor vehicles and other human-related activities were causing the acid rain. The resulting precipitation was killing the lakes and other aquatic systems in Scandinavia, Europe, Canada and the U.S., including the Great Lakes. It was clearly in everyone's interest to make sure our freshwater lakes weren't going to die, and the International Joint Commission (IJC) got involved to fix the problem.

The IJC was created by Canada and the United States to manage their shared water systems along the border and is guided by the Boundary Waters Treaty of 1909. The acid rain phenomenon went away after the Canada–United States Air Quality Agreement was signed in 1991, forcing industry to upgrade facilities and pollution standards. Coal stacks today trap almost 99 percent of the material coming from these plants and acid rain is largely a thing of the past. Making polluters accountable for their business practices is just one aspect of corporate responsibility.

Another worthy cause was cutting gas emissions from cars. That came about partly as an economic reaction to the oil crisis in the 1970s, when OPEC cut supplies to get the world price up. But it probably was a good thing in its own right. It was done over time, and the automakers chipped in, making lighter cars, following more exacting emissions standards and ultimately improving mileage and lowering the cost of operating the vehicles. Not only have those improvements been beneficial for consumers, they've also been good for the environment. And it all began as a response to economics.

To take corporate responsibility seriously, companies must not only react and respond to pressure from governments, regulators and consumers, they need to be aware of the issues that are important to their stakeholders and to society at large, to understand the implications of their decisions and business practices on the environment or the local community, and to be proactive about encouraging sustainability and stewardship. The corporate community, in fact, has to be part of the pressure for positive social change.

That was my thinking on corporate accountability at the time I retired in 2007 — and remains so today to some extent. I've said before that I'm a big proponent of doing the right thing first and foremost, and I was worrying about companies that we supported or invested in walking the wrong side of that line. Obviously, as with South Africa's apartheid regime, that had been the case in several notable instances in the past. Of course, we had changed the way we did things when made aware or called out, but how could we get ahead of all that to be even more responsible corporate citizens?

Corporations are faced with a huge range of ethical dilemmas and complex challenges that come with doing business in a global marketplace. What I'm asking is how does a corporation — a bank such as BMO — manage that stress being put on you to be good current corporate citizens while also protecting shareholder value? Whether it's your corporate policy and practices, your choice of investments and trading partners or your environmental footprint, how does any organization balance its business goals and priorities with the impact it inevitably has on the broader community?

That's a very difficult challenge. As head of an organization, you're going to be asked about these kinds of issues all the time. You're going to be challenged and your organization is going to be challenged. So how do we balance concern about the environment with concern for the shareholders of the Bank? These difficult questions about complex challenges are made more difficult by the twenty-four-hour news cycle. Social media never sleeps. You may decide to think over an issue overnight only to find that social media has decided it for you by the time you wake up in the morning. That's not inconsequential, because even if you've got a successful business and you're doing the right kinds of things, you can still get beat up. The minute you start feeling defensive, you're seen by the media as admitting guilt.

So what would my advice be to the current CEOs? Speak whereof you know, is my own philosophy. Don't just try to mouth the beliefs and phrases of everyone who has a loud voice in media or society because it seems like the right thing to do. Speak what you know and speak what you think is the right thing. (As Mark Twain said, tell the truth and you'll never have anything to remember.) Sometimes, as CEO, you've got to have chutzpah. You've got to stand up to the critics and advocate for what you believe is the right thing.

Authenticity and communication are key to this effort. As I've said, these can be very complex issues and the public, the media or the stakeholders that are calling you out don't necessarily understand all the factors at play or the implications of certain decisions. As CEO, it's your job not only to stand up for what you think is right for your organization but also to communicate effectively to the broader community why what you're doing is also right for society in general. That's what happened in the wake of the non-merger with RBC: we had many loud voices in the media and in the business telling us what they thought we should do. It would have been easy to get lost in making them happy and catering to their interests, but we ultimately stuck to what we knew and what we were good at.

I can be braver now that I'm retired, that's true. But I have always tried to stand by my principles. A good example is Indigenous rights in Canada. The Bank has been active on the file for a long while. In 1992, we created a Task Force on the Advancement of Aboriginal Peoples in the Workforce, just as we had before for the advancement of women. And we backed that up with our hiring of Ron Jamieson as the first Indigenous executive in the bank. Long before most other major organizations were sensitive to the issue, we at BMO felt it was important to be as inclusive in our employment and business practices as possible.

MLSE chairman Larry Tanenbaum recalls our activism on the file: "I was at a dinner at the Bank, and Tony had arranged for Ron Jamieson, the first senior Aboriginal banker, to be the speaker. Ron spoke about some of the things that I'd never really focused on that concerned our Indigenous communities here in Canada. I knew of the poverty, but I didn't know about how they couldn't get mortgages on a home on a reservation because of a law that says, 'You don't actually own that piece of land. It's owned by the reservation.'"

"Tony moved to make changes to bring our First Nations people into the world of business and banking. And it really woke me up to the idea of working with the Indigenous community and seeing what we could do. Today, at MLSE we're partnering on a number of projects with Indigenous communities because of what Tony introduced us to back at that time. Ron Jamieson went on to help build economic bridges to the First Nations people and is still very active in that effort."

But let me be clear that standing up for what you think is right does not necessarily mean reacting to every influence that pressures you. You sometimes have to set aside the demands from outside groups in the interest of fairness, to stand by your principles or to do what you know or believe is right for your organization. As a small example, in my position as the co-founder of FAST (Fighting Antisemitism Together), we had people coming to us all the time asking us to support their causes. I said that if we started making political statements, the regulators could challenge our charitable status for espousing issues outside our stated purpose. They'd have auditors all over us. I insisted that we were not in the business of politics; this was all about our purpose, the FAST organization, and about education specific to our cause.

I used those same guiding principles of speak-what-you-know and do-the-right-thing on a daily basis at BMO. For example, when investors would come to me and say, "We've got this hot new product. It's a deposit product, and we are going to guarantee it based on the return on the shareholder."

I would say, "What happens if the stock market drops? That's a big risk. It's certainly a concern. We're guaranteeing the investment, but we didn't guarantee the downside? That's not the right thing to do."

"Yes, but nobody says that we can't do that. Technically."

My answer to that kind of response would inevitably be, "Get out of here." Once you begin looking for loopholes and substitute your principles for "no one says we can't do that," you'll never succeed in the long run. We dodged a lot of trouble by avoiding what everyone else was saying, doing or getting away with. The more important question is, "What's the right thing to do for our business, for our stakeholders, for the community?"

That's an important guiding principle and I've always lived by it. Do the right thing. And remember that not every issue is black and white, either. There are many levels of nuance to everything, there is room to satisfy people without adopting extremes. Now, maybe you get it wrong sometimes. And if you're anticipating the whims of social media, you're sure to get it wrong. Maybe your idea of doing the right thing is different from somebody else's morality. But the right response is always: first, to do the things that are required by law, which is the bare minimum of doing what's right; second, and more importantly, do things that seem to make sense from the point of view of both the business and the common good.

TONY'S TAKEAWAY

Your view of doing the right thing isn't necessarily always going to conform to everybody else's view of doing the right thing. But I always found it a pretty good standard, and it made me feel like I could sleep at night. Corporate accountability is a dance between doing what's best for the business in the framework of what's best for society. Find a healthy balance that benefits both. And don't apologize for speaking what you know.

CHAPTER 14

An Economic Imperative: Why Supporting Communities Benefits Everyone

It stood thus in our stars when we were born;
The long and short of it is this: Endure."
— GEOFFREY CHAUCER, *The Canterbury Tales*

In my career at the Bank I was often asked, why do some businesses fail and some succeed? After all, only six stocks listed on the present-day Dow Jones Industrial were on the list in 1976. I had seen so many companies come and go, I suppose people felt that gave me some perspective on the subject. There's no simple answer, of course. For instance, I'm always fascinated when I drive along Bloor Street in Toronto and notice which businesses thrive and which end up shutting their doors. That's the way the market economy operates, I suppose, but why is one enterprise a passing fancy, just the flavour of the month, and another a lasting fixture in the neighbourhood? As I look at them, I'm always thinking about how companies connect with not only their customers, but also their community — and in some cases, even how cities can grow around a business.

You can make an argument that the Stratford Festival — and by extension the City of Stratford, Ontario — exists the way it is today because of a connection with Bank of Montreal. Stratford in the 1920s was a centre of furniture manufacturing in North America. It sat right near great arboreal forests of white ash, oak, maple, walnut — all the best wood for furniture and even hockey sticks. But the industry collapsed during the Great Depression. Demand for furniture in the

1930s fell dramatically. Later, with business cratering in the 1950s, the railroad pulled out. People were desperate. Stratford was on the verge of becoming a ghost town.

Tom Patterson was a local entrepreneur and journalist who had always had the idea of creating a festival theatre to produce the plays of Shakespeare in his hometown. After World War II, he looked at the state of the city and wondered how he could make his idea a reality. And in the early 1950s, as other businesses in the area were struggling, the Stratford Shakespeare Festival, as it used to be known, was born. Patterson helped hire Sir Tyrone Guthrie, the noted British actor, director and producer, as its first artistic director.

But getting it off the ground took money, of course. (For the first few seasons, the stage and auditorium were under a tent. It wasn't until 1957 that the Festival Theatre opened, with its permanent stage based on Shakespeare's model of the Globe Theatre in London.) In the early days, Tom asked around and found little luck. Finally, the local Bank of Montreal manager advanced him $2,000 to get the Festival started in 1953 — we've been their banker ever since. That branch manager not only gave away two thousand bucks on loan, he also shared Tom's vision that this was an investment in the community, a way to re-energize the economy of the town. Now, Stratford is a thriving city, revolving almost entirely around the arts.

So, the question arises, how does a bank justify a loan to help create a community arts initiative? Pretty simple, from my perspective. I've always believed we can never be more successful than the communities in which we live and work. As "Canada's first bank," we do business in and support thousands of communities across the nation; in fact, BMO was a factor in the birth of many. But simply handing out money without a plan is not in the Bank's mandate. Rather, using our resources, skills and advice to support initiatives that foster the well-being of communities, as well as supporting and enabling economic growth and prosperity, is in our interest, and the interest of our shareholders, many of whom through their pension funds are owners of BMO.

There has to be an economic justification for contributions to hospitals, schools and other foundational aspects of local communities. Why?

They create jobs. Jobs produce taxes. Taxes enable the funding of the healthcare system that we have. That is why it's not just a "good thing" to support hospitals, schools and local initiatives, it's an economic imperative. So, back to Stratford, in that case it was a triple benefit: to help local business and grow the Bank, while also helping the common good.

Now, there have been a couple of examples where this kind of thing was contested. In 1923, there was a case launched against Bank of Montreal in Quebec saying that it was inappropriate for us to make a donation to a Montreal hospital — the argument was that shareholders' money should go to the shareholders only. After the Bank won the case at a lower level, it went all the way to the Quebec Superior Court. The Quebec Superior Court, however, correctly understood the rationale for this type of social benefit. They ruled that it was totally appropriate for the Bank to do this. At the time, this legal argument established that it was acceptable for the Bank to make this kind of charitable donation because the shareholders trusted the board of directors to act in their best interests and on their behalf. This seems like such a normal part of doing business today — that companies can do with their earnings whatever they deem worthy, within limits — but it had not been the norm before this 1923 case.

So, what's appropriate? Are too many corporations chasing virtue and then trying to somehow later justify the business case? I see that too much now. In fact, there is a dangerous trend that I don't agree with — that is, putting the social cart before the economic horse. Thomas Piketty, French economist, neo-Marxist and author of *Capital in the Twenty-First Century*, believes that capitalism inevitably leads to increasing inequality and excess wealth accumulation among the top 10 percent of the population.

I am disturbed over the increasingly common notion promoted by Piketty and his disciples — like the Organisation for Economic Co-operation and Development — that capitalism is broken and irrelevant in modern society. For instance, the *Financial Times* did an entire edition asking whether capitalism is dead, pointing to social inequality and societal dissatisfaction as the reasons corporations must change the concept of shareholder value. I couldn't quite believe it — the venerable

Financial Times, a bastion of capitalism, espousing this sentiment. Thank goodness *The Economist* came out squarely and said, in effect, this is nonsense.

Thankfully, we are now seeing research from the Urban Institute in Washington that shows statistics debunking Piketty's claims of rampant inequality. Writes Terence Corcoran in the *Financial Post*, "Piketty has said that the top 10 percent of Americans had walked off with between 50 and 100 percent of U.S. economic growth between 1979 and 2014. The actual number [of their share] is much lower." Piketty also once claimed that the median income in the U.S. (which statistically captures the middle class) had fallen by 10 percent during the same decades. But other studies, including one from the Congressional Budget Office, actually show an increase in median household income of up to 50 percent.

Returning to the notion of corporate social conscience, in his book Piketty also questions the legitimacy of individuals, primarily CEOs, espousing a social cause. He's even questioning the fact that noted ultra-rich business leaders like Bill Gates invest the billions of dollars that they've earned to do good things in the world, such as fighting malaria, polio, poverty and other social maladies. That seems to be a wonderful thing, but Piketty questions whether these successful people are just using that money to assuage their own feelings of guilt after accumulating so much wealth thanks to their employees and average customers. I think the term now is virtue signalling: "I'm a good guy because I'm giving all this money away. In the meantime, I exploited the economy to do it." In any case, that's the argument in Piketty's book.

So let's ask the question: Is fighting malaria a good thing for a corporation to do? Of course it's a good thing. It's a *wonderful* thing. But is it appropriate to allocate shareholder resources for a personal cause using company funds? The distinction I use — this may sound like self-aggrandizement and I don't mean it to be — is to ask if what you're doing is really economically advantageous to both the shareholders and citizens. That, to me, is the integration of social liberalism, which I favour, with fiscal conservatism, which I align myself with as well.

In this memoir I talk a lot about the contribution that corporations can make if they follow a policy of doing the right thing. If, as I said, we can never be more successful than the communities in which we live and work, it's in our economic interest to financially support the arts and hospitals because it makes our communities healthier and more economically vibrant. And we all win as a result. Stratford is an excellent example of this philosophy coming to fruition.

So how does a corporation strike a working balance between benefitting shareholders and benefitting society? Let's do a thought exercise.

Imagine the chairman of the board of a major corporation sitting down with the CEO and explaining to him or her why they've just been fired. "Look, over the last eight quarters, our stock prices have gone nowhere. Market share is dropping, and we are cutting back on costs."

The soon-to-be ex-CEO then says, "But you don't understand. I've been focusing on improving the lot of our employees and helping them live better. I've been focusing on our customers — our customer service scores are up."

The chairman says, "Let me explain something to you about improving the lot of our employees and helping them live better: we've got 30,000 employees. Based on our commitment to shareholder value, and creating shareholder value, I've had them heavily skew their pension funds into stock in this company. By dropping the ball on increasing shareholder value and today's profit performance, we are endangering their financial futures. You know what you've done to the pension fund of our 30,000 employees? You've jeopardized it. If our shareholders aren't receiving dividends, they aren't paying taxes — which pay for all these social programs they'll need in retirement. By the way, where are your measures of how their conditions have improved as a result of your focus? Do you have specific goals and measures? How are they going to relate to shareholder improvement? Sorry, but that doesn't cut it." End of story.

Everyone knows the counterarguments about not investing in society. You hear it every day when someone rails about robber-baron capitalism. What's less known is the impact of shareholder value to society, which no one talks about because it's not fashionable.

Another way to see this balance between shareholder benefit and societal benefit is to look at the advancement of women in business and the program we started in 1990, which we looked at in detail in Chapter 12. At the beginning of our efforts I said to Matt Barrett, "This is an economic issue for us. If we have an undervalued resource that we're under-leveraging, think of what tapping into that is going to do for shareholder value." I said, "Oh by the way, it also has a wonderful knock-on social benefit, in terms of equality and bringing women along in the economy."

As mentioned earlier, we won the Catalyst Award in 1994, and the policy was picked up by Bill Downe and then Darryl White as they became CEOs of BMO. The Bank won the Catalyst Award again in 2018 and now the reforms we made have become widespread in the industry. The world is waking up to the fact that the underrepresentation of women in positions of authority is not a just a social issue; it's an economic one as well. Equity for women has a socially beneficial impact *and* it is a generator of economic wealth. In my opinion, any corporation that says they're implementing such an initiative — or any corporate social responsibility initiative, for that matter — because it's the right thing to do, and that's their *only* reason for doing it, is not sufficiently justified in taking it on. It's got to have an economic justification as well; first, because our primary responsibility is to the shareholders, and second, because doing good things for economically sound reasons brings benefits for the social good along on the backs of them.

We took the same kind of approach when we promoted the recommendations of the three subsequent task forces focused on members of visible minorities, Indigenous people and people with disabilities. We talked about maximizing our strengths as an organization and seizing the corporate advantage by being leaders. What I soon discovered, however, is that I could have come at it the other way and the message would have been just as effective. The "right thing to do" was reason enough, at least for BMO people.

So don't believe people who tell you that social issues are incompatible with capitalism or that the terms are mutually exclusive. By growing the talent pool and human capital of the Bank, we improved the lives of our employees and our stockholders and brought benefits to the community and Canadian society at large.

TONY'S TAKEAWAY

We can only be as successful as the communities in which we live and work. Corporations have an opportunity, even a responsibility, to strengthen the communities in which they do business by using prudent investment. But it must not be done at the expense of shareholder value that funds so much in society.

VOICE: **KAREN MAIDMENT**

Karen Maidment joined BMO as chief financial officer early in my tenure as CEO. She elected, with my full support, to commute daily from Cambridge, Ontario, one hundred kilometres from Toronto, but never missed a beat. She was a trusted and valued supporter and partner, a key contributor to our journey to the creation of a significant shareholder value. She remains a close friend to this day.

I first met Tony in 2000 when BMO was looking for a chief financial officer. I had been approached for the job, but at the time I wasn't really looking for a change. In addition, I didn't have a lot of interest in joining a bank. But I went to meet Tony anyway. I was very much expecting a formal and quite traditional CEO who would spend most of the time talking about his needs and the Bank's expectations.

Instead, I met a person who was very interested in what I had to say, someone who wanted to hear my story and who was interested in working with a new leader from outside the Bank, whose career had brought them different experiences. I was intrigued. However, I also had young children and I simply did not think I could pull off a move to Toronto and make it work for my family. Again, to my utter surprise, Tony raised the potential for a non-conventional work arrangement. In the end, that's what we did, and I think it's fair to say it was not only highly successful, but it also provided an example for others to follow.

And that's Tony. At times, he does come across as quiet, conservative and formal. But the lasting impression for me, and many others, is of a deeply thoughtful, gracious and caring person. He's also forward-looking to the point where I don't think it's an exaggeration to say he's a visionary.

While his business expertise and performance are well known, I want to share some thoughts about another aspect of his business orientation that reflects his personal values and underscores his vision.

In the early 1990s Tony, as president and chief operating officer of BMO, created three important internal task forces on the advancement of women and other underrepresented groups at the Bank. The goal was to understand and act upon the question of how best to unleash the capabilities of people and groups whose talents and potential had not been sufficiently recognized or taken care of in the world of work. The Task Force on the Advancement of Women reported in 1991. This was a landmark report and was unusually candid about the perceptions and realities of contemporary women bankers struggling to move forward in financial institutions, as well as the solutions needed to start making change.

Years later, I experienced first hand Tony's undiminished passion for diversity and the benefits it brings to corporations and society, as he continued to walk the talk. This was highly unusual at the time, when most leaders just talked.

CHAPTER 15

Rebranding a Legend

If gold rusts, what then can iron do?
— GEOFFREY CHAUCER, *The Canterbury Tales*

B MO. What's in a name? I like to ask people if they know what BMO stands for. Where did our new name come from? (Insert *Jeopardy* music here.) Simple: BMO is the bank's symbol on the stock exchange. But nobody knows what it means. They all think it means Bank of Montreal. And it does — in the financial world!

There were a number of considerations that went into switching our brand from Bank of Montreal to BMO. I remind people that all things are an evolution — a gradual one. As I said in the outset, *festina lente* — make haste slowly. So the change from Bank of Montreal to BMO was not something that suddenly happened in a flash in 2002. The complete rebranding of a major enterprise is not something to be taken lightly. By the time we officially adopted the change, we had been talking for years about the BMO branding strategy.

The need for a change to our corporate identity was something that had been bugging me, unarticulated, for a long period of time. We were too defined as being associated with Montreal and Quebec. Of course, that was our heritage; that's where the company was founded in 1817 and where our head office officially remains to this day. (And my own Québécois heritage gives me a strong personal attachment to Quebec and Montreal. Our family on my maternal grandfather's side goes back to 1667, when my ancestor Mathurin Dubé came to New France.)

But the nerve centre of the Bank, as it were, the operational head office, was moved to First Canadian Place in Toronto in 1977. In the years after the move, not only was the enterprise functionally based in Toronto, but we were also becoming an international organization. The old moniker was never going to work for us moving forward.

On the other hand, we couldn't just willy-nilly drop a name that for over 175 years we had built as our brand. The public can be very fickle about these things, even when it comes to banks — which is ironic because the banks are typically stereotyped by the general public as the epitome of big business in this country. We get blamed for many things, rightly or not. But it's like anything else: my own doctor's a saint, but the medical profession is not. Similarly, the banks are kind of reviled on the one hand, but they are respected within their own community. They represent stability and prosperity and the manager is a trusted advisor, a figure of financial wisdom. It's like we hate the banks — but they are *our* banks. As Canada's oldest incorporated bank, we had to be very careful about shaking up our identity.

In fact, the whole notion of rebranding Bank of Montreal to BMO was one of the more delicate issues I had to deal with as CEO. We began asking, how much was having "Montreal" in the name a limitation in terms of our expansion into other markets, particularly the U.S., and even in the mindset of Canadian consumers? Most people do not realize that the Royal Bank started as a Halifax bank. Nobody knows that. And most people don't know that CIBC, the Canadian Imperial Bank of Commerce, with its national-sounding name, got its start in Toronto. Did we want to respect the past and remain linked in name to one city, a province, even a country? That was more my own thinking than anything else. I liked the name; it had recognition. But was that identification with a specific geography a thing of the past in an increasingly globalized world?

We learned a funny thing about our attachment to the city of Montreal. According to our research, the Bank of Montreal brand was as important in English Canada as it was in French Canada. That reflected the cross-cultural board of directors back in 1817. This was a coalition of smart businesspeople, French and English, and two Americans. They knew that we needed a local made-in-Canada financial institution, not a British spinoff or something from the United States. We needed to bring it home and have our own financial system, so they clearly, obviously and *intentionally* put that nationalist stake in the ground with the Bank of Montreal name. But it was always about Canada.

By the twenty-first century we were talking about losing the word "Montreal" entirely. I wrestled with this decision because your brand is something you don't want to tinker with too much. How do you get the best of both worlds? How do you keep the link to the memory, the connection to where you came from and the vision of the founders, and not just turf that out totally? How do you do that and still move forward into the future?

There had been precedents for this kind of massive rebranding in the world of Canadian banking. Toronto-Dominion Bank had become TD Bank, moving away from the original name by the 1980s. (I've heard what bothered them more was the *Dominion*, not the *Toronto* part of their name.) The Bank of Nova Scotia goes by Scotiabank now, although the place name is still embedded in their brand. And Royal Bank of Canada has moved on to become RBC. All the banks that switched titles did so around the same time as we did — and for the same reasons. We were all acquiring businesses in the United States and beyond and couldn't be perceived as simply local Canadian banks any longer. Our customer base was international, and the market was global.

Our rebranding efforts coincided with a number of acquisitions we had made in that period. In 1984 we had bought Harris Bank, based in Chicago. Bank of Montreal in the United States? You can just hear Americans say, "What's that all about? That doesn't work." (Coincidentally, we also started to move away from Harris Bank as an identifier in the larger U.S. market, for all the same reasons. Harris Bank was a very strong brand in Chicago and in Illinois in general. So we kept that name for a while, even though it was a hard pill to swallow. However, we've been moving away from that in recent years. It's now BMO Harris Bank.)

So, we were reluctantly driven to lose the old names. And the issue became, what do we call ourselves? We started kicking this around, thinking about how we could bridge our future with the past, keep the connection to the history, make it more contemporaneous and modern and not throw the past away. But at the same time we needed to lose some of the geographic specificity. Even if the name on the outside changes, the values inside had to remain the same.

That's where we came up with BMO. It was a good combination of something that already existed, that was well known to anybody in the securities business. It may not have been as well-known right away to people at large, but we decided to transition by using "BMO Bank of Montreal." Even to this day you'll see that specific branding on a lot of the retail branches. Also, using this format in the branding of other parts of our business, such as BMO Capital Markets, would help to spread consistency in our identity and familiarity with the name.

In 1995, I started working with people from Ove Design. I'd known Michel Viau, their founder and past president and CEO, for thirty-five or forty years, and the firm still performs design work for the Bank's annual report and the FAST annual report. We kicked the new BMO brand around a lot, trying to decide on the new look: how to bridge to tradition and create a contemporary visual identity that would work for the future and in many different configurations in our various businesses. We played with many ways to do it until the BMO red roundel emerged — that was my innovation — which unified the concept. You now see it everywhere: BMO Financial Group, BMO Capital Markets, BMO Wealth Management, BMO Harris Bank, BMO Asset Management and, most ubiquitously, BMO Bank of Montreal throughout the retail branch system. All connected by the red roundel.

Internally, we had to sell only one person on it, and that was our CEO, Matt Barrett. Once he was onside, the rest just flowed naturally. We had also been bringing our board along through the journey, and they enthusiastically endorsed our approach. And quite a journey it was, beginning on Matt's watch and extending into mine, with the official changeover coming in 2002 when I was CEO.

After we had struggled internally through the long exercise of rebranding and had sorted out our new corporate identity, rolling it out was fairly easy. Outside the Bank there was only a little resistance. We started the rollout slowly, and then we started to use the new branding gradually, rather than taking a big-bang approach that would potentially confuse and unsettle consumers.

The rollout was helped by a few other factors too. By that point we were starting to modernize the physical design of the branches, so this was a golden opportunity to introduce a new visual identity at the same time. The brand-new branches looked all shiny and contemporary, everything clean and polished, and with a new logo: BMO Bank of Montreal. For the people who had long identified with Bank of Montreal, that name was still there. You could ignore the BMO if you liked. Younger people and people who were familiar with the securities side, on the other hand, preferred the shorter, more succinct name. So it was this double banger. More than anything else, the new branding, and the new look of the branches in particular, probably worked on a subconscious level to communicate to people that we were an established organization with a long, proud heritage, and modern and technologically savvy enough to thrive in the rapidly changing business environment.

As for the person on the street, either they didn't care — which is in all likelihood the case — or, seeing these kinds of changes going on all around them, they might have thought, "Oh yeah, all these corporate guys, they're always coming up with some jazzy new thing." It was not just us. From Apple to Procter & Gamble to Google, nearly everyone was coming up with some contemporary branding and marketing. In this flurry of visible corporate change, there was almost an expectation that we upgrade the name and the look. When people would ask me about the name change, whenever I would be doing a presentation or on the street, I'd just say, "It's the branches being modernized; we're just becoming more contemporary." It happened as easily as that.

As I've said, we could only be as successful as the communities in which we lived and worked. And a key part of that community-building was done through our growing corporate sponsorship of sports and the arts. Supporting local teams, venues and artistic groups became a major part of enhancing our identity in cities and regions across the country.

With the growth of television and the rise of digital media, sports had become big business with massive fan bases from across a wide cross-section of society. We had to be there, and we were, identifying with the strong emotional connections Canadians have to their best-loved teams and sports. Our sports sponsorships started with the Montreal Expos in 1969, back when BMO corporate headquarters was still in the city. *Le Grand Orange*, Rusty Staub was the big star, and with him as the symbol we had the Young Expos promotion, where the kids could sign up to belong to a fan club sponsored by the Bank. People were just crazy about the Expos as Canada's first major league baseball team, and that became kind of a natural marriage of sport and city.

Later, our affiliation with Toronto FC was another interesting application of the brand to their new stadium at the CNE grounds. Maple Leaf Sports and Entertainment (MLSE) owned the team and the chairman, Larry Tanenbaum, was a good friend of mine. We had worked really hard together to explore ways of marrying our brand to soccer. I would bump into Larry at a dinner, and he'd say how wonderful it would be for BMO to support TFC and their brand. But the way I thought about it was all about the opportunity for BMO: "You know what goes along with this sponsorship package? This big sign that's going to sit there right on top of the Gardiner Expressway. And every car that passes by is going to see 'BMO Field.' And it's on 24/7, twelve months a year, flashing away, whether there's a team playing on the pitch or not."

We extended our support of major league soccer to the Montreal Impact as well, and what goes along with the package for both teams is the European concept of featuring the sponsor's branding on the players' jerseys. There's nothing like seeing the BMO logo on the jersey of a goal scorer, in TV coverage or in the sports section of the *Toronto Star* or *Montreal Gazette*. It's great for the BMO brand to be associated with positive moments and caught up with the emotion of the fans. In the grand scheme of things, this kind of marketing is not that expensive and it goes a long way to supporting goodwill in the communities in which we work. I'm also proud to say that we have made a big commitment to soccer at the grassroots level as well, supporting more than 100 soccer clubs across Canada. It always puts a smile on my face to see the BMO logo on the jerseys of young girls and boys playing soccer in communities across the country — some 18,000 kids in all.

Our former CEO, Bill Mulholland, was very big as a horseman, which is how we ended up being involved with the world-class Spruce Meadows equestrian facility south of Calgary. When Ron Southern — from energy, logistics and construction giant ATCO — put the arm on Bill to be the principal sponsor for the dressage events at Spruce Meadows, that was the start of a stronger attachment to Calgary, which was really starting to boom in the energy business (and where my grandparents had settled after moving from Marengo, Saskatchewan). And we shouldn't overlook BMO's commitment to Skate Canada over the years, either.

We've also given major sponsorship to arts organizations over the years, including Canadian Opera Company, the National Ballet of Canada, the Royal Winnipeg Ballet and the Stratford Festival. To some, this might be a little less intuitive and a little more controversial than the sports connections. You may ask, "Who goes to the opera and the ballet or to watch Shakespeare? How do we bond with these types of audiences?" Well, lovers of the arts are just as passionate about the organizations they support as sports fans are about their teams. Where in sports you have people from all economic strata, in the arts, most hardcore fans are from higher-income households, so the obvious connection there tends to be more for the wealth-management segment of our services. Its appeal may be a bit more restricted, but it still has a very definite and devoted audience.

Some people might wonder how supporting the arts is a good use of the Bank's money if those followings represent maybe only 5 percent of the population. The audiences may be sparse compared to a stadium full of people, but their value is substantial. For example, part of that 5 percent of the population supports the whole city of Stratford, Ontario, and all the people that work there, including all the people who serve tables and have hotel rooms and so on. And all those people and all those businesses pay taxes, which then go back into the community to support social programs and more.

It's notoriously tricky to do a critical analytical market evaluation of the impact that any one of our sponsorship programs has on our bottom line. That goes for all marketing and advertising. The impact is very difficult to measure in tangible ways, so we look at these programs from the perspective of branding and community-building. To me, the arts are an essential part of the intellectual life of the community, part of the educational fabric of the community. I really believe that strong support for the arts creates a healthy infrastructure from which everybody benefits. Investing in that intellectual capital rebounds to not only the health of the economy, but ultimately the growth of the economy and social benefit.

Support for the arts by BMO also means supporting the local economy, if you will; artists are part of the economy just as much as any businessperson. That's why we are lucky to have Dawn Cain curate our collection and inform our support for artists in the local communities in which we are present. As part of BMO's commitment to young Canadian artists, she helped initiate our 1st Art! program, in which a jury chooses exemplary works by young art students, giving them a hand up in establishing careers in visual arts.

A lesser-known kind of support for the arts lies in BMO's collection of paintings, sculptures and other visual arts. When we buy works of art to put into the branch in Guelph, we look for a Guelph artist. When you go across Canada, to Edmonton and Wetaskiwin, you'll find works in our buildings by local artists there, reflecting the community in which they work. And in Chicago, you'll find works by local artists hanging in our buildings there. Supporting local artists also makes some of our collection available to the public. No, it's not seen by as many people as would watch TFC in the MLS final, but it does support the artistic endeavours of artists and, in a broader sense, the intellectual life of our country.

TONY'S TAKEAWAY

As Chaucer wrote in "The Pardoner's Tale," "Radix malorum est Cupiditas" (greed is the root of all evil). The modern corporation that neglects its civic responsibility while pushing profit above all cannot succeed. The BMO roundel is more than just a branding mark for the Bank. It also represents our organization's values, including the investment we make in our collective culture, education and heritage — not just wealth for its own sake, but investing in a society that's made better for everyone in it. For that reason, the rebranding of Bank of Montreal to BMO, and everything it stands for, is one of my proudest achievements at the Bank.

VOICE: **DAWN CAIN**

*Dawn Cain joined BMO as curator of the Bank's collection
of art. In addition to transforming the approach to managing
our valued collection of historical works, she, in short order,
built one of the finest collections of contemporary art in
the country. Dawn was very close to my wife, Liz, and is
curator of our personal collection as well as being a valued
advisor on art matters. With her help, we have supported
a number of Canadian artists both past and present who
deserve greater attention.*

I was working at the University of Toronto and curating some smaller
projects when I was told that Tony Comper was interested in discussing
the art collection of the Bank of Montreal. It was an extensive collection, but the Bank had not really had it properly curated. Mr. Comper
and his wife Liz were very interested in art, and they had a substantial commitment to, among other things, the art of Canadian women
painters.

I was asked by Orde Morton, BMO's vice-president of Editorial
Services and Government Relations, to come to Tony's office at the
Bank shortly after he retired in 2007 to discuss what he wanted to do
with the impressive collection BMO had amassed over the years. Tony
and I chatted about the many pieces the Bank had assembled and what
might be done with them. I could tell that he was serious about art, and
that he saw it as important to him and the Bank. He showed me a few
paintings he had in the office and asked about whether they should put
title plaques on the frames. I said, "No, the practice is to put a title on
the wall next to the painting." After the meeting, I was walking to the

elevator, and someone said I shouldn't have contradicted a bank president like that. I thought, "Oh well, I guess I blew it."

But that wasn't what happened at all. Tony called me and said he wanted to talk about my proposal for BMO 1st Art!, which would celebrate the creativity of art-school students from over one hundred postsecondary institutions across Canada. And he said let's go ahead with this program that would give financial support to artists under forty.

And so we have done that. And from these early meetings with Tony, I have made curating the BMO collection my life. He doesn't try to oversee every detail. He gives you the outline of what he's looking for and he trusts you to do the best, because you're the expert. His commitment to art and its place in business is genuine, and he's a true supporter of Canadian artists.

CHAPTER 16

Diversification: Andrew Jackson's Folly, Canada's Blessing

Shepherds too soft who let their duty sleep,
Encourage wolves to tear the lambs and sheep.
— GEOFFREY CHAUCER, *The Canterbury Tales*

A s I said in the introduction, diversification is a hallmark of BMO that sets us apart. To help understand what diversification means, bear with me as I give some context. Diversification is just one dimension of risk management, arguably the most important function for all banks and financial institutions — and in that I'd also include governments.

Large banks, like Bank of Montreal, are engaging in many businesses, the majority of which involve financing the Canadian economy and the economies of other countries, as well as the economic activities of their customers and of the bank itself. One major aspect of a bank's business involves the assumption and management of risk to effectively conduct these financing activities, and in advising customers in the management of the risk associated with their own personal and business financial activities.

Assuming and managing risk has many dimensions in itself, a large part of which is diversification, and there are in turn many dimensions to that. Suffice it to say that this is all complex stuff, but getting it right is fundamental to the creation of shareholder value and to the functioning of the economy overall.

A defining feature of Bank of Montreal's "getting this right" is its industry-leading, consistently superior performance on this measure over thirty years. Careful, indeed splendid, construction of Bank of Montreal's risk management architecture during the decade of the 1980s, under the leadership of Bill Mulholland, has resulted in BMO outperforming all other Canadian and international banks over thirty years.

A few examples from our past, both good and bad, will help bring risk management to life. In 1894, two banks in Newfoundland failed. The economy of Newfoundland was primarily concentrated in the fishing industry, and a downturn in that and other factors precipitated a financial crisis. Bank of Montreal and two others were brought in to take over and manage the banking system. As a result, Bank of Montreal soon assumed the government account. Why did those Newfoundland banks fail? It was unavoidable — the economy was not diversified enough.

Lack of diversification was also why there was a huge wave of consolidation in the banking industry from 1890 to 1920. The Home Bank, the Bank of Toronto, the Molson Bank — they weren't diversified and got into trouble being concentrated in one economic region and one geographic region. They all got bought up by the bigger banks, and their rescue again shows the importance of diversification.

It takes a long time to build a highly diversified financial system in a country like Canada. As Canada's oldest bank, we were fortunate in that we got started before anybody else did, and we had invested in the Canadian Pacific Railway. So we got going across Canada long before any of the other banks had a chance to get into the market out west. Geographical diversification meant that if there was a financial meltdown in one part of the economy, BMO was backstopped by its other investments. And we were blessed that circumstances have allowed the Bank's holdings to become further diversified in many sectors across Canada: energy in Alberta, manufacturing in Ontario and Quebec, farming and fishing in so many provinces. We learned early that diversification reduced our risks. Geographically, and by industry segment, diversification is the most important risk mitigant in the banking business.

That said, you still have to be able to assess your risk on an ongoing basis. How can you tell that too much risk is tied up in a single source?

How will you cope if the stories the investors tell you about diversification turn out to be false? Is it too good to be true? The failure of Calgary's Dome Petroleum is a good warning tale. Everyone seemingly had a piece of Dome's financing in the 1970s and '80s. When the price of oil dropped in 1986, many financial institutions discovered that putting all your eggs in that one basket is a perilous gamble. The credit crunch nearly sank some of them who'd bet heavily on Dome. More recently, a lack of diversification led to the 2008 economic collapse, predicated upon packaged mortgage sales and derivatives in other nations.

This is why any business must know itself and its environment when assessing its strategy. One of my abiding principles is don't impute motive in risk propositions that seem too good to be true. Focus only on the behaviour you're seeing. Sometimes you may want to think about where somebody's coming from or why they're behaving a certain way, but the best advice is often to look at what's before you. You don't know what goes on in other people's minds. You don't know what's going on in their personal lives. And you don't know what's going on in the C-suites and boardrooms of other companies. Don't play amateur psychologist when it comes to risk management — especially in big deals.

A lot of people worry that there is too much concentration in the Canadian banking system with just five or six major banks; however, my theory is that their very size is what gives them such strength individually and the sector such strength overall. Their size allows them to stay diversified and manage risk effectively. The Canadian banking system stands in stark contrast to the U.S. system, where there are literally thousands of smaller banks, most locally based. And all thanks to Andrew Jackson.

I know my colleague Bruce is a big believer that Andrew Jackson was one of the most significant U.S. presidents of all time. He might have been. But he did one thing that was a big mistake, planting the seeds for the demise of many financial institutions in America, when he decided to cancel the charter of the Second Bank of the United States in 1832 (it took till 1836 for the bank to completely dissolve). He was worried that Alexander Hamilton's model for the nation encouraged the growth of big eastern banks that would dominate the economy. Conceptually, he was not wrong. Jackson was a Tennessean, and with western expansion, he wanted the economy to be more locally based. Cancelling Second Bank's charter ultimately led to having as many as 14,000 banks in the United States (it's down to around 6,000 now). Think of that: 14,000 locally based banks with almost zero diversification. Until relatively recently, the State of Illinois allowed only one branch of each bank in the state.

Jackson's plan was that no single bank would grow too big to monopolize the financial system, and the result is that today, there exists a basic contradiction in the U.S. financial system: the Americans made banks smaller so that they wouldn't grow too powerful, but they also made them vulnerable to credit and liquidity issues. Take Continental Illinois as an example. It was a big business — one of the top banks in the world. What they would do is raise wholesale funding at the money markets to fund more growth. The minute there was a credit crash or a liquidity crunch, all the wholesale lenders were pulling their paper. That's why CI went broke — their source of funding was very, very fast moving, and there was zero diversification.

On the other hand, retail deposits stay forever; they don't give a worry about whether or not their deposit is going to go sour. That's stabilizing; that's diversification. Most banks don't realize that. But when you have to depend on money markets, you're prone to being caught short. Diversification is a key element of risk management for Canadian banks.

So if good risk management is so important, why doesn't everybody do it? Because when you have a booming economic growth period, there's a lot of pressure to take risks. Even your own guys, who want to compete for business, are saying, "That guy down the street is sticking his neck out, he's lending way over the top. Why shouldn't we?" Well, it's not apparently risky at the time, so the loans seem fine. But when the cyclical economic factors of that economy go sour (as they did during the COVID-19 crisis) those who take more risk get killed on loan losses. And that's when we conservative lenders win.

Because of our relatively conservative risk profile, BMO was not as exposed as other banks when the economy took a downturn in 2003 or 2008. The advantage — which most people don't realize — is that, yes, our customers might miss out to some degree in a short run of strong economic growth, but they will experience less downside in a market downturn. Managing risk at BMO is about being around for the long run, always there for our customers through thick and thin. Although we won't necessarily be the most aggressive at the time of great economic expansion, we don't back riskier prospects. As a result, some of our customers, not all of them, would rather deal with Bank of Montreal because it will keep them out of trouble. That means as much to the average Canadian investor as it does to the CEOs of some bigger companies who don't want their guys to go nutty on risky projects and investments everyone else is chasing. They like the security we offer.

As another example, in the mid-2000s, derivatives were the big deal among investment banking guys. They were hot to trot over this new financial instrument, and everybody was into derivatives. Some Canadian banks even set about to be the big player on Wall Street in derivatives. I remember Matt Barrett saying to me, "I really hope they're successful. But we're not going to touch it, because we don't really understand the risk, how it can go wrong, and how it can be messed up." He was happy to let go of the Trojan Horse of derivatives. And, of course, the whole thing collapsed.

I can't speak for the competition, but at BMO we were able to withstand that enormous 2008 financial collapse because of one thing: diversification. Unlike the U.S. banks, the large Canadian banks were able to have the best of both worlds: big enough to be diversified and manage risk effectively and yet have an entrenched local presence at the retail level. We were both on the world stage *and* able to serve local communities effectively. Andrew Jackson was only able to see one side of that picture.

There's a great banking story that illustrates the key difference between the Canadian banking system and Jackson's concept. It may be apocryphal but, still, it's a great story. Amadeo Pietro Giannini founded the Bank of Italy in 1904 to cater to the Italian immigrant population on the U.S. West Coast. (It became known as the Bank of America in 1930.) Then something interesting happened. He travelled to Banff on holiday and went into the local Bank of Montreal branch — he was intrigued by the concept of the Bank of Montreal *in Banff.* How, he asked the branch manager, does this work? How does the head office control this local branch in Banff, a zillion miles away from Montreal?

Well, the branch manager handed him two maroon-coloured binders, each five inches thick, one with A–L on the spine and the other M–Z. These were called the routine circulars, the routine procedures and instructions that told this manager many miles from Montreal how to run the branch. (And this is where I'm getting old enough to remember, because routine circulars were still around in my day.)

This branch out in the Canadian wilds wasn't just a well that whipped out money — it was guided by head office with strong processes and controls for everything from foreign-exchange procedures to interest rates and how to manage all kinds of bank business. So Giannini reportedly said, "That's very interesting." He went home to California and modelled the Bank of America on that concept of branch banking under a centralized federal office.

In fact, the California banks were relatively bulletproof from the Andrew Jackson concept, because California was a big enough state and its economy well diversified so it didn't have the same risk as if it depended solely on one or two economic sectors. Even a so-called "local" bank could be very big and diversified and have lots of branches. Wells Fargo and Bank of America are the two biggest examples.

But nothing works better than the diversity built up over generations by Bank of Montreal and other Canadian institutions. The COVID-19 pandemic was the latest example of the challenges the global market economy can face. When the history of the virus' impact is written for Canada, I'm confident that our backstopping the economy will play a large part in re-emerging from the dark days it visited on the nation.

TONY'S TAKEAWAY

Sometimes, you can afford to stand aside while others take great risks or gamble on a lack of diversification. As I've said in this chapter, that can be much tougher than it looks. But in the long term, it provides stability and shareholder value to your customers. Canadians can be thankful the Andrew Jackson banking "miracle" never made it north of the U.S./ Canada border. It has made Canadian banks a paragon of diversification and sober risk management.

VOICE: **ROB PRICHARD** oc, **PART 2**

When Tony was appointed as Chairman and CEO of BMO, my wife and I hosted a dinner in his honour at our residence, the University of Toronto president's house, gathering friends and colleagues closest to Tony. We set up one large table with about forty seats for the dinner, which included appropriate toasts and congratulations to our guest of honour. But we wanted to make it a memorable evening so, unbeknownst to Tony, we worked to reassemble his band, The Compleat Works, from his university days.

Near the end of dinner, his former bandmates arrived and began playing a set as the guests all started to dance. With a bit of encouragement, Tony was persuaded to join them and took his place with his guitar (a bass, I think) and played the set. It was fabulous: Tony, the newly minted, strait-laced corporate bank CEO reverting to his rock and roll youth, showing a side of himself almost no one knew and proving again what a multidimensional and multitalented person he is. We took lots of pictures that evening that should be available in the university archives, if they are not in Tony's personal collection.

CHAPTER 17

Is Executive Compensation Out of Line?

We know little of the things for which we pray.
— GEOFFREY CHAUCER, *The Canterbury Tales*

I have been asked, "How do you answer the criticism that bank executives are paid too much?" It's an interesting question, and one that is
getting much discussion these days. One of the reported "sins" of market
economies that is most frequently cited is the growing difference between
CEO "salaries" and those of the employees who work for them. And the
supposed indifference on behalf of those CEOs for people with less.

First, let's establish that the term "salary" is somewhat misleading
when, in fact, we are really discussing "compensation." A CEO's remu-
neration comprises stock options, bonuses, benefits, executive perquisites,
long-term incentives and other components in addition to base pay. Why
is this worth noting? As the largest component of executive compensation is not tied to salary but to equity and shareholder value, this
compensation is based, principally, on the health of the business being
run. Growth in salaries means the corporation is growing, generating
income and wealth for everyone — including employee pensions and the
retirement income of individuals invested in the stocks of such companies (something rarely mentioned in these discussions). This produces a
concomitant increase in taxes paid, which helps to finance health care,
education and other social benefits. Receiving equity as a key part of
the compensation package keeps a CEO focused on the health of the
organization's bottom line, which is good for everyone. I know this may

sound self-serving to some, but in my opinion we should promote robust CEO compensation for the reasons I mentioned above — because it means growth in compensation for everyone within the company.

Before I get to the specifics of my own situation, let me take a step back to address the reported divide between executive compensation and the middle class. In my view this has become a societal issue partly because of the regression-to-the-mean phenomenon in our economy that you see discussed in books such as Thomas Gilovich's *How We Know What Isn't So* (discussed in Chapter 6). That is, the assertion that middle-class wage growth has not been what it was in the late 1940s and the 1950s, even as CEOs are setting records for compensation.

Some have been saying recently that we must now re-order the wealth proposition in society to restore the great hope of the 1950s, when everybody was doing well, middle-class salaries were growing and so on. Everybody who was willing to work had a chicken in the pot, it seemed. Now, middle-class prosperity has allegedly pulled back and regressed to the mean just as millennials are entering their peak earning years in the job market. Wage growth is not what it once was. Technology is changing the work force. These voices — and not a few political aspirants — are talking about the U.S. primarily, but it also applies to Canada.

So what happened here?

Well, I ask my questioners, which economic pattern was the exception? Today or the post–WWII period? In my opinion, the huge economic growth spurt of the late 1940s and the 1950s was an exception largely caused by the massive destruction of Europe, North Africa, Japan and parts of Asia in World War II. Europe and Japan in particular were destroyed, and the reinvestment required to rebuild those societies was unbelievable and unprecedented. The Marshall Plan came along, guaranteeing the rebuilding and flowing resources into the economy.

Meanwhile, there were virtually no dishwashers made for personal use in North America from 1941 to 1945. Same for dryers. Domestic automobile production slowed to nothing till after the war. Industrial production had gone into the war machine. Then, it had gone into the recovery and rebuild of war-torn nations. When that ended around 1947–48, the recovery in North America finally benefitted the consumer. A huge explosion of economic growth was fuelled by returning servicemen and -women who now wanted to settle down and build a home and a family. They had money stored up. There was pent-up demand with nothing to spend it on until the late 1940s.

My dad used to finance the retail appliance industry in Toronto in those days. Dad said business in 1948 was a laugh — they couldn't keep up with the sudden surge in demand. The store owner would just stand at the front door and the customers would say, "We've got a new house, and we need a washing machine and a dryer." And the store owner would reply, "Fine, I'll put you on the waiting list." Eight months later you got your machines — if you were lucky. Once the factories got really producing domestic goods again, that backlog was cleared up. But there was still a huge demand for consumer goods. The surge helped fund the creation of a working middle class that was involved in building those cars, homes, appliances and other consumables for families starting up after the war. Unions helped lock in the prosperity for a time. Families could live on a single income.

Soon, the standard was two cars in every garage, not one. Tiny black-and-white TVs eventually became sixty-inch flat screens. Bunkbeds gave way to queen-sized beds for everyone. Homes went from one bathroom to one for every occupant. The new "normal" was more extravagant than the *Leave It to Beaver* standards. But it's important to remember that this postwar era has been atypical by historical standards. That spectacular growth was not sustainable forever in the face of escalating demand and consumer requirements. At some point demand peaked. Now we have regression to the mean. In addition, you've got hugely improved productivity due to automation; humans are losing jobs now being done by machines or computers. We haven't seen the end of it yet, and there's going to be unrest in this transition. Those "lifetime" jobs we took for granted fifty years ago are fast disappearing — and the replacement jobs are not apparent yet. This is reported to have caused a crash in expectations in the middle class, particularly in the Gen-X and millennial cohorts.

Naturally, some politicians exploited the shift in expectations. In 2011, Senator Elizabeth Warren famously summed up the societal unrest: "There is nobody in this country who got rich on his own — nobody. You built a factory out there? Good for you. But I want to be clear. You moved your goods to market on the roads the rest of us paid for. You hired workers the rest of us paid to educate. You were safe in your factory because of police forces and fire forces that the rest of us paid for. You didn't have to worry that marauding bands would come and seize everything at your factory — and hire someone to protect against this — because of the work the rest of us did. Now look, you built a factory and it turned into something terrific, or a great idea. God bless — keep a big hunk of it. But part of the underlying social contract is, you take a hunk of that and pay forward for the next kid who comes along."

Barack Obama famously (and effectively) repeated this mantra while running for president in 2012, with his "You didn't build that" remark. Both he and Warren were promoting the notion that public funds are essential to the creation of wealth. It sounds nice, but it's not how the market economy works and how money is distributed. Private enterprise creates wealth. Government redistributes that wealth. And all the public speeches in the world are not going to change that.

Certainly there is inequality between the pay of senior leadership and the average employee, but, says Vincent Geloso of the Fraser Institute, "Some people exaggerate the extent of CEO pay relative to the pay of the average worker by using 'apples-to-oranges' comparisons. For example, they compare the cash pay of all workers to the total compensation of the top 100 CEOs and arrive at a ratio of 197 to 1. But a much more instructive apple-to-apple comparison — comparing the total compensation of the top 1,000 CEOs (the maximum number available in databases) with the workers in the firms managed by those same CEOs — dramatically shrinks the ratio of CEO-to-worker compensation by 81 percent."

The vast majority of tax revenue comes from the Canadians who create wealth. A 2017 study by the Fraser Institute showed "the top 20 percent of income earners in Canada — families with an annual income greater than $186,875 — will . . . pay 55.9 percent of all taxes including not just income taxes, but payroll taxes, sales taxes and property taxes, among others."

Furthermore, compensation for bank executives is not a giveaway. We do have market forces in play, and when investors are interested in shareholder value, that's the price you pay for that kind of production. If it's simply a given that banks produce prosperity *ad infinitum* and anyone can do it, ask those shareholders and retirees how they felt when the management of BMO saved them from the excesses of the 2001 Enron scandal, the 2001-02 dot-com collapse or the 2008 derivatives mess that collapsed banks in the U.S. and around the world. Surely running a bank is more than simply wearing a suit and approving mortgages.

There is also criticism that Canada shouldn't have these levels of executive compensation with its smaller market. To answer this point, I would point to my counterparts in the United States who earn, on balance, somewhere between 40 to 70 percent more than the equivalent Canadian CEOs do. Same global market, same job descriptions, same risks. My compensation was a reward for me getting the Bank to perform at an international level at which we created a certain level of shareholder value and profit, and, therefore, we also paid more taxes, which in turn could support more of the infrastructure and social programs and things of that nature that we value as a society.

For comparison about compensation, let's look at the world of professional sports. Players are making huge amounts of money. We had a standing ovation for DeMar DeRozan the first time he came back to Toronto after his trade to San Antonio in 2018 (where he was signed to a five-year deal guaranteed to pay him $137.5 million). The same people cheered Kawhi Leonard when he came back in 2019 after rejecting Toronto for a better contract in Los Angeles. Sure, $103 million over three years is a lot of money. And why? Because Kawhi is a rare commodity. That's the price NBA teams have to pay for the scarcity of talent at that level. If you look at the European soccer leagues you'll see the same thing: the top tier of athletes, stars like Lionel Messi and Cristiano Ronaldo, can make $50 million a year. And why? Because of the return those clubs are going to get from the TV rights, merchandise and logo and digital rights.

The counterargument to that comparison might be, "Yes, but the NBA players only play until they're thirty-five or so; they've got to make a lot of money now. And they have the star power to fill an entire venue; if they said Tony Comper were appearing tonight at the Scotiabank Arena, there'd be crickets."

Although that's true, I did have to fill a metaphorical stadium — the annual shareholders' meeting — and that is a very large cohort, one that collectively — through funds and institutional investors — and individually, held 639.2 million shares. That may not be as high-profile as a sports team filling the Scotiabank Arena or the Rogers Centre, but it has a very wide-reaching effect across the economy that touches on the retirement income of millions of Canadians and the investments of young families.

Now, to continue with our sports comparison, look at the value creation in major-league teams. Franchise equity has gone from millions to billions in the pro sports leagues. Maybe they should pay their CEOs four times what they do now if they're going to generate that kind of shareholder value. Why? Because the company's going to make more money and generate more in contributions to the community in the form of foundation grants and general tax revenues. So, get on with it, I say.

The average person doesn't seem to worry about the outrageous amounts of money paid to Hollywood stars, either. It's okay for Tom Cruise or Denzel Washington to be wealthy as long as the customer is entertained? Why is the standard different for the CEOs and other executives who not only create wealth for themselves, but also provide jobs for millions of employees and contribute substantially to the common good through the personal and corporate taxes they pay, donations to charitable causes and educational institutions, sponsorship of the arts and other causes and much more?

A final observation: Today's young people, in general, seem to be pessimistic about whether the market economy still works. In no particular order they cite the gap between the 1 percent and the average worker; the climate crisis; income disparity; the prohibitively high cost of buying a home and now the long term impact of COVID-19. My response to their concerns is, if there's one message to take away from history, it's been humankind's fabulous creativity in overcoming its problems — and how they, too, can be part of the next wave of innovation and creativity. Even in the face of adversity, opportunities arise, just as they will from the global crisis brought on by COVID-19. As entrepreneur, sports owner and TV star Mark Cuban said at the heart of the pandemic, "When we look back in five years, we are going to realize that there were ten to twenty amazing companies that were started that changed the world and led us to a brighter future. Ask yourself: 'Why Not Me' or 'Why Not Us.' Now is your time. The world is waiting."

Here's a historical example of what Cuban means: In the early 1900s, there were hundreds of thousands of working horses in a city like Toronto or New York. They had too much horse manure in the streets and the dried manure blew around and got into the water supply, causing respiratory ailments and other diseases. The people at the time were perplexed by how to solve the problems. And then, within ten years, humankind had the automobile — and they'd solved their manure problem.

A classic example of perception distorting reality is the Club of Rome's predictions for the world economy. In 1972 an article in the *Atlantic Monthly* reported a study on sustainability conducted by the Club of Rome. This intellectual think tank predicted that the world was going to run out of basic natural resources such as iron, oil and copper. They used statistics to show that mining and drilling for oil and other resources were causing them to rapidly run out, and the 1973 OPEC oil crisis seemed to confirm their research.

But those great shortages didn't happen. The world continues to extract all these commodities today and will do so well into the future. So what was the flaw in this study? Well, one thing is it didn't account for innovation. The authors' predictions were based on "economically proven resource recovery," getting at these resources according to the status quo and not accounting for the development of new technologies. For example, after a burst in technological innovation America is currently self-reliant on fossil fuels. (Canada is another story.) What these kinds of developments show is that creativity and ingenuity — often led by the corporate class in tandem with the public sector — can work to everyone's benefit.

Personally, I would not have been able to support the causes and charities I wanted to in my personal life without the resources I earned from creating shareholder value for millions of shareholders. Generous compensation and personal wealth have also enabled people like Bill Gates and Paul Allen to spend billions of dollars doing good that isn't being done by national governments, the United Nations or any political entity.

If I might also add, investing in the banks themselves has been very beneficial not just to CEOs but to many Canadians' RRSPs and savings. A BMO share in 1983 was worth $6.4375; in 2019 that share was worth $89.56 — a 1,226.82 percent increase when inflation averaged just 2.15 percent a year. Roughly speaking, the same kind of increase goes for the other Canadian banks. Show me another investment that rewards investors to that degree, to say nothing of the contribution made to government tax revenues.

TONY'S TAKEAWAY

The market system can often seem unfair and capricious. But to paraphrase a dictum attributed to Winston Churchill about common-law jurisprudence: "Capitalism is the worst economic system — except for all the others that have been tried."

CHAPTER 18

Globalization, or the Law of Comparative Advantage

It seems to me that poverty is an eyeglass through which one may see his true friends.
— GEOFFREY CHAUCER, *The Canterbury Tales*

If many blame capitalism for the ills of society, as we saw in the last chapter, it seems many today want to blame globalization specifically (as just one aspect of capitalism) as one of the causes. On issues from the COVID-19 pandemic to diversity, globalization has taken a hit lately. On the other hand, an equal number still consider globalization an engine of prosperity. Who is correct? And who benefits from it?

First of all, globalization is a nebulous term to me. It sounds good, has the ring of authority, but it doesn't begin to scratch surface of a complicated concept. These days globalization has come to mean a thousand things for a thousand different people. As it's understood today in the most general terms, it could broadly mean capitalism-fuelled trade.

I prefer the more specific term Law of Comparative Advantage: "someone will produce more of and consume less of a good for which they have a comparative advantage." To me, that explains the huge economic expansion that has occurred in the world economy over the centuries. Not just in Western civilization — Western Europe, North America and to some degree in South America — but also in Japan and, increasingly, in emerging markets, thanks in no small part to the massive economies of China and India joining the world. It's the triumph of classic market capitalism.

To a large degree, the economic structure of the global economy as we know it today began with people doing the right thing, irrespective of how they were criticized. The most prominent example is General George Marshall's proposal to rebuild Europe after World War II. The Marshall Plan faced huge opposition within the U.S. government, including from President Harry Truman at first, but Marshall persisted, and out of the destruction of World War II came huge expansion, particularly the economic growth and prosperity of North America.

But there were larger benefits beyond that. Many countries started looking outward to trade partners: How do we get our products into the world? How does the world access our economy? And Marshall's vision, more than anything else, brought about the formation of the World Trade Organization and the starting of the General Agreement on Tariffs and Trade (GATT) rounds, allowing for some of the biggest evolution in world trade in history.

It began well before Marshall, of course. If you go back and read all the great economic philosophers of the seventeenth and eighteenth centuries — writers such as Thomas Paine, whose pamphlets inspired the American Revolution, and back to Thomas Hobbes in *Leviathan* and Adam Smith in *The Wealth of Nations* — the birth of modern economic theory proposed outward-looking policies. Smith's book was significant because he sought to discover what made some countries of the time wealthy and some not. His conclusion? Trade. An openness to the world distinguished Scotland and England and Holland and made them into global powers. Those who rejected the world outside their boundaries never achieved the same measure of success.

Even in Britain, outward-looking trade policies were not always the order of the day. For example, the protectionist British Corn Laws of 1815–46 were at entirely the opposite end of the spectrum. The Corn Laws safeguarded the landowners from the importation of competing goods and services. They limited fair competition and were essentially a rejection of the outside world. Eventually, however, the free traders won the day, and the Corn Laws were repealed.

Despite episodes such as the Corn Laws, the British Empire was for centuries the hallmark of globalization. Based on its military, naval and commercial prowess, the British were running the world in the latter part of the nineteenth century through rapid expansionism and enormous amounts of trade with their colonies all over the globe. India, Africa, the Caribbean, North America, the Far East — the sun truly never set on the British Empire.

But globalization wasn't confined to the British. In Lisbon, for example, the huge St. Jerome monastery was built entirely on the riches that came from the cinnamon trade. Portugal naturally became a trading nation, with outward-looking princes such as Henry the Navigator (Henry the Alligator as we used to call him in high school) and Lisbon, the coastal capital, facilitating trade. Way back in 1494, the Treaty of Tordesillas had divided the New World between the Spanish and Portuguese empires, the two colonial superpowers of the time. The French, Dutch and other European nations went on to do empire-building of their own and all of these colonial powers, along with the British, blazed the trail to globalization as we know it today.

(South America is a good example of what happens when you shun globalization. Argentina in 1907 had virtually the same-sized economy as the United States. What happened? The country installed protectionist policies. They turned inward and away from global trade; now, their economy is still forever needing to be saved, because it isn't diversified. Conversely, I think the U.S. is the most successful economy in the history of the world and will continue to be.)

The fascinating thing to me is not simply the benefits of globalization but how they extend far beyond economic wealth. It's not just about the rampant spread of capitalism (nor is that a bad thing). For with the trade of goods comes the export of culture and of art as well; as economies grow, so do entire cultures thrive and evolve.

One of my fascinations, as you may realize by now, is medieval studies. I've never really seen much work outside of Georges Duby's writing on the subject of culture and trade in the medieval period, but I find his thesis intriguing. Prosperous civilizations have thrived not only through their trade or manufacturing but their flourishing culture. For example, the ancient Greeks were a military and economic power, trading throughout the world known to them at the time. They also had one of the richest cultural civilizations in history, with playwrights and artists and poets and philosophers whose work and influence survives to this day.

My fascination about those civilizations is how did they develop that investment in culture? It couldn't be done by merely surviving and scratching out a living. A civilization, or nation, needs to prosper economically before it can develop culturally. There has to be an economic underpinning that allows people to invest time and energy and thinking into a broader perspective than simply grinding corn and pounding rocks. Author Marion Turner talks about that transformation of culture in her book, *Chaucer: A European Life*: "Without the [economic] changes of thirteenth- and fourteenth-century Europe, the kind of visual art that Giotto made and the kind of poetry that Bocaccio and Chaucer wrought could not have been produced. Chaucer . . . was perfectly poised to become the poet of the counting house."

That's a realization, I think, of the good that comes from allowing capitalism to flourish and improve a society's economic circumstances, which then allows the culture to develop. Neither the Great Pyramids in Egypt nor the temple complexes of Angkor Wat could have been possible if the population was concerned exclusively with putting money in their pocket. Yes, of course, slave labour and war and subjugation of the enemy were contributing factors to many cultural wonders such as these, all unacceptable to modern eyes. But, something more facilitated that kind of massive infrastructure building — a higher urge to serve spirituality and to create.

What were the economic factors that allowed that to happen, and are they similar to the economic factors that allowed the rebirth of Europe under the Marshall Plan and the creation of global trade organizations and agreements, such as the World Trade Organization and the GATT?

Look at the way culture developed in Europe. Go back to the time between the tenth century and the mid-thirteenth century and the great medieval warming period from 950 to 1250 AD. Hundreds of years of inordinate warming allowed an unprecedented expansion of crop growth and a corresponding reduction in mortality in Europe. As a result, labour demand skyrocketed and wages went up, justifying the resources now available to build cathedrals and produce great art and scholarship. It's just the way economics works. Labour is scarce because there's so much more crop land. How, then, are we going to harvest it? Pay the workers more. Huge growth ensues, and the minute your wages go up, you started to become capable of doing other things than just ploughing the land. And serfdom disappears. A middle class — the *popolo* described in Turner's book — emerges. The pattern is there all through history and across the globe.

But what really fascinates me is, if globalization is so great, how did it become a bad word? How did it become a pejorative? It probably happened in the twentieth century when some of the growth factors started to turn against the pattern that had developed over hundreds of years before. As I've explained in Chapter 17, the media and others blame "income inequality" (the gap between the ultra-rich 1 percent and the average taxpayer) on globalization and rampant capitalism. They also assume that the post–World War II economy was "normal," when the economy boomed, the middle class flourished and income spreads tightened from 1950 to 1980. What we are seeing now — those income spreads widening again — is likely a regression to the mean. Whether that means income inequality or not, concentration of wealth has existed for much more of recorded history than it has not.

What should we consider as normal, then? Well, no one can say precisely. If you listen to Steven Pinker — cognitive psychologist, linguist and bestselling author — he'll tell you that this current period of reversion to the mean, with income spreads widening again, is a moment on a much larger historical screen. That if you look at broader economic trends, humankind continues to evolve on a generally upward trajectory, which is good. It's positive — as Martin Luther King said, "The arc of the moral universe is long, but it bends towards justice."

However, that progress requires perspective. It takes sufficient time and sample sizes. Let me illustrate that with a simplistic banking analogy. Being a teller is the most boring, unproductive job in any bank. (I know firsthand, having done it early in my career.) Talk to any teller. Having to punch the same transaction on a machine for eight hours a day is boring. Few who've done it would recommend being a teller. But there was still pushback when banks largely eliminated the position. The media decried job losses. Yet what did the tellers become? They were retrained and became financial advisors. They moved up the food chain. They began doing different jobs that were more intellectually stimulating. And they developed more skills, which these employees could leverage if they went into the broader job marketplace.

That's not a lot of help to the guy in Oshawa who was just laid off because GM is eliminating shifts at the local plant. I realize that. But the larger point here is that we shouldn't resist the influences of globalization in order to preserve the status quo of boring jobs and stultifying occupations. Research shows that what makes people happy at work isn't more money but creativity, the respect of peers and a feeling of belonging most of all. There is going to be a huge challenge in creating those kinds of jobs while eliminating the menial ones. It will be the great challenge of this century, converting the workforce to new work positions. But if we look at the evolution of tellers to advisors and other skilled jobs, you can see a pathway the banks have created.

Globalization has also allowed us in the Bank to contemplate expansion in other markets. It changed and diversified our business, making it stronger because it provided us with a window into opportunities other than our home market. In our case, BMO is growing like crazy in the United States, particularly the Midwest. Now we're making almost more money in the United States than we are in Canada. A couple of years ago our current CEO, Darryl White, said that he was going to see the U.S. earnings be 40 percent of BMO's total earnings. He said it was going to take five years. He surpassed that prediction in six months.

Outside North America, we've been invested and interested in Asia since the nineteenth century. Now we have a huge wealth management business there. (I hate the term wealth management, but nevertheless, we're the biggest Canadian player in that area in Asia.) Going global is not a new thing, and it's critical to building and maintaining our strength as a leading Canadian enterprise.

While many see globalization at the macro level, some of our strongest growth in recent years has been in the small-business sector. We financed and published a report on women-owned businesses in Canada about fifteen years ago. It was unbelievable in terms of opportunity. Now that we have unleashed the power of women and invested in them, they're responding. A whole segment, 50 percent of society, has been opened up and empowered to perform. Now, you've just doubled your capacity for economic growth. Yes, the small businesses we invest in, whether run by women or men, are based in Canada, but they are doing business on the world stage and tapping into other economies. That's another example of globalization and free markets operating.

The investments that Canada has made in education have also made it a real global talent resource. The Greater Toronto Area, for example, has become a centre of excellence in artificial intelligence, with the highest concentration of AI startups in the world. Corporate investments in this area and others benefit the economy and Canadians overall through the growth of jobs and trade opportunities in emerging technologies. In 2019, BMO invested $5 million in the BMO Lab for Creative Research in the Arts, Performance, Emerging Technologies and AI at the University of Toronto, the Bank's largest gift ever to a single Canadian institution.

And in the same year, Gerry Schwartz and Heather Reisman gave a record $100 million to create the new Schwartz Reisman Innovation Centre, focused on innovations in AI, biomedicine and other disruptive technologies, and to support the launch of the Schwartz Reisman Institute for Technology and Society. Investing in the country's human capital is nothing new for Canadian corporations and entrepreneurs. The Perimeter Institute for Theoretical Physics, today a leading centre for scientific research, training and education outreach, was founded in 1999 by Mike Lazaridis, one of the BlackBerry founders. Based in Waterloo, Ontario, the Perimeter Institute, like other Canadian centres of excellence, contributes to the country's intellectual capital and attracts leading researchers, academics and thinkers from around the world. This can only be good for our economy and our reputation on the world stage.

Overall, the education infrastructure in this country is fantastic. Our universities, such as U of T, McGill, Western and UBC routinely rank competitively with the best in the United States and Europe. And the University of Waterloo routinely gets raided by Amazon and Google and all the Silicon Valley crowd. Our educational institutions and their graduates are a global asset that will allow us to trade with the world to the betterment of more people.

What could go wrong with all of this is protectionism — the same thing that happened in the 1930s. That cutting-off from the world — and between provinces — at that time was a reaction to the perceived harm of global capitalism during the Depression that led to displaced populations, financial ruin and flirtation with extreme political movements. Make no mistake, protectionism is dangerously just around the corner, largely because globalization has allowed the Chinese economy to come close to being on equal footing with the U.S. China is manufacturing products for the world market that are cheaper for the consumer than others can supply. That's impacting the American consumer and American workers. Not surprisingly, Americans feel threatened by China becoming their economic equal, and they are turning to the remedy of tariffs and trade wars to fend off the wave of globalization lapping on their shores. And suddenly, the global crisis of the COVID-19 pandemic has forced the global community in general to think and act differently about supply-chain markets, perhaps encouraging a new level of protectionism the world over that we could not imagine happening.

That's catastrophizer Tony talking. I don't really think that's going to happen, because the U.S., and the midmarket customers in the U.S., know that in the modern economy they need the rest of the world more than ever before. They'll figure out ways to modify whatever protectionist regulations are imposed. They'll have to find new ways around them. And they will. It's too small a world not to embrace the opportunities.

TONY'S TAKEAWAY

Back to our question at the beginning of this chapter: who benefits in globalization? While the COVID-19 pandemic has shown the vulnerabilities of open trade, there is also much to suggest that we have all benefitted over the passage of time. The Greeks knew something about all this years ago as they expanded the known world, and we are wise to listen to their lessons.

CHAPTER 19

Crisis Management: Withstanding Storms Requires a Firm Will

Yet from the wise take this for common sense,
That to the poor all times are out of joint
Therefore beware of reaching such a point.
— GEOFFREY CHAUCER, *The Canterbury Tales*

I watched with interest how the financial industry handled the COVID-19 crisis that emerged in late 2019. It was truly a challenging time in every way as leadership had to balance grave health issues with the potential collapse of the economy. What made it unique was that it was not caused by economic factors but by a health crisis. Its vast implications are barely understood at this writing, but I hope the lessons of earlier crises will serve to guide those responsible for the recovery, or for the management of a future crisis of any scope.

In my time as a senior executive at Bank of Montreal, there were four periods of crisis that required some exceptional management skill as well as luck to survive. One of them was, of course, the 1998 "merger that never was" with Royal Bank (covered in detail in Chapter 2). Before that there was the real estate crash of 1990, and after it was the 2001–02 dot-com bubble collapse. And then there was the derivatives crisis in 2008, which occurred immediately after my retirement in 2007. How are they the same and how are they different? And how did BMO manage through all of these periods of crisis and disruption to avoid the pitfalls that tripped up other banks?

The 1990 crash was a general economic depression, but the big raw factor in it was a collapse in the real estate market in Canada. Why? First, because the banks were being too aggressive at lending for construction projects. That's why the banks have now got something called the 75 percent rule; in other words, today developers have to have achieved 75 percent financing of their project through pre-development sales before the banks will finance the project.

Before the 1990 crash, banks would finance 100 percent of the project, and then the builders would undertake their sales. If they didn't sell enough, then they'd go bankrupt. Nowhere was this more common than in the condominium market. For example, builders would have obtained bank financing for condominium units each worth, say, $400,000 on the market and could raise only maybe $300,000 on average per unit, which wouldn't even cover what they owed the bank. Before they were finished the loans were underwater. That all changed after 1990, and since then fewer condo projects have gone bankrupt, because the banks are no longer lending on speculation. They will finance a project only when the developer comes to them with at least 75 percent of the financing already in hand.

The second factor in the 1990 crash was on the retail side. You hear about a thing called the gross debt service ratio (roughly the proportion of the gross debt obligations you would be paying each month while owning a particular property). In my day, it would be 37 percent. So, if your gross debt service ratio was north of 37 percent, we wouldn't lend you the money for the mortgage to buy the house. You had to have a gross debt service ratio lower than 37 percent, including the cost of the mortgage (although most borrowers with good credit and a reliable income will sometimes be allowed to exceed these guidelines).

Many of these retail loans were also made in anticipation of changes to zoning in the hotter markets in Canada that would boost the value of the investments. People were often spending the anticipated appreciation before it ever was realized. When those changes didn't happen, investors were left underwater and the properties went bankrupt. According to betterdwelling.com the average sale through the Toronto Real Estate Board (TREB) was $273,698 in 1989. "Over the next seven years, the average price dropped and finally bottomed in 1996 at $198,150.

If you bought at the peak, and sold at the bottom — you lost $75,548, or roughly 27.6 percent of your purchase. It took thirteen years for the average price to recover in Toronto."

When the developers failed and large parts of the residential market collapsed, the banks found themselves holding a glut of properties and having to carry a number of buyers until the market rebounded (which it eventually did — and then some). Notwithstanding this, the Canadian banks weathered the storm. Other financial institutions were not so fortunate and found themselves eventually out of business or absorbed by the large banks. The banks survived in large part because the big Canadian banks are very conservative, and so are most of their customers.

In fact, do you know where we have our lowest loan losses, historically, through thick and thin? The Atlantic provinces. You don't think of that intuitively, but they're very conservative people because the economy has been a slower growth economy. They're not buying the next big hype. This is Tony's philosophy, not necessarily substantiated by fact and science, but acquired through contact with the borrowers in the Atlantic provinces for many decades. Real estate remains a very aggressive commodity in other parts of the country, but the forces fuelling the growth — outside low interest rates — are more external rather than internal.

The 2001–02 dot-com bubble crash was the next major disruption to the financial markets and the next huge challenge we had to manage during my tenure at head office. The rise of the internet in the late 1990s and the e-commerce phenomenon created an explosion of opportunities and bright ideas. All of a sudden, entrepreneurs everywhere had found a way to tap into the global market. The upside was endless — or so they thought. It was the classic entrepreneurial mentality at work, but on a grander scale than ever before: with your money and my brains, we'll do wonderful things. Good for them if they could find someone else to finance their dreams. That's what all these dot-com entrepreneurs were looking for, and the investment community was all too keen to get caught up in the excitement of what looked like unlimited opportunity.

From my perspective at BMO, all these guys on the covers of business magazines acted as if they'd invented this new way of doing business. Three smart guys, one from Harvard, would come to my office at the Bank and pitch the latest dot-com concept, looking for investors to lend them $100 million to finance their dream. And lots of banks, angel investors, private equity finance and others got on board in a big way. Everybody was into these science-fiction companies that had zero customer revenue. It was all a concept, an idea, a wonderful thing — and many in the financial industry thought they'd better get in on some of that action before the markets discover what's going on.

For me, this was where my software-development background came in. I'd receive these people in my office with their great pitches and they'd think, "Who's this old guy? What does he know about this hip technology?" I'd hear them out, and then simply ask, "Where are the revenues? How much have you budgeted for the complexity of this software?" Suddenly the smiles disappeared. They had met someone who wasn't buying their dream scenarios. And then I'd kick them out of my office. Our Bank was largely spared the worst of the collapse in investments as a result.

What they were in fact doing was creating a massive bubble in the market. The dot-com craze and the companies that drove it were seductively attractive propositions, but they were mostly ideas and dreams built on nothing — zero sales, zero results, just endless opportunity and upside. Where were these fantastic expected revenues actually going to come from? How do you measure the potential of a whole new kind of business model no one has seen before? But there was so much temptation in the investing community to get in on the hype and get a piece of the action that many turned a blind eye to the risk and all the questions and jumped on board.

During the dot-com bubble, the technology-dominated Nasdaq index rose from under 1,000 to more than 5,000 between the years 1995 and 2000. In 2001 and through 2002, the bubble burst, with equities entering a bear market. According to investopedia.com the crash "saw the Nasdaq index, which had risen five-fold between 1995 and 2000, tumble from a peak of 5,048.62 on March 10, 2000, to 1,139.90 on Oct 4, 2002, a 76.81 percent fall. By the end of 2001, most dot-com stocks had gone bust. Even the share prices of blue-chip technology stocks like Cisco, Intel and Oracle lost more than 80 percent of their value.

It would take fifteen years for the Nasdaq to regain its dot-com peak, which it did on April 23, 2015."

Of course this wasn't the first time in history that investment mania had reached fever pitch over an asset that simply was not there. The dot-com crash wasn't the first bubble to burst, and it won't be the last. Tulipmania occurred in Holland in the early to mid-1600s, when tulip bulbs were reputed to be trading as high as six times the average person's salary. (It's a good story about the concept of some commodities getting overblown, but it's mostly untrue.) The South Sea bubble that burst in 1720, ruining many British investors in an elaborate hoax, was probably a better example as a comparison, but nobody really wants to understand that one.

It could turn out to be the same sort of phenomenon with Bitcoin and other cryptocurrencies. There's no real substance behind them. Everyone's applauding the idea until someone loses $290 million dollars, and then lenders are going, "Oh, who's going to bail us out? What about the regulations?" The point is, if you're investing in companies and commodities that you don't understand, you're more likely to get burned. As Warren Buffett has famously advised, "Never invest in a business you cannot understand." And another oft-quoted corollary to that, also from Buffett: "Risk comes from not knowing what you are doing." But it's hard for many investors to resist the temptation to get in on the hype.

Finally, there was the global financial crisis of 2008. The biggest financial collapse since the Great Depression of 1929 was fuelled by speculation on real-estate derivatives and led to the Great Recession as capital dried up around the world. The Big Short, as Michael Lewis called it, was a very serious situation for the entire financial industry, and many investors — the ones who survived it — are still feeling the aftershocks from it. As we know, legendary financial names such as Bear Stearns and Lehman Brothers disappeared in the process. Small nations such as Iceland had to be rescued from bankruptcy. The U.S. estimated that as much as U.S. $9 trillion dollars was added to its debt over the decade following the financial crisis. In the first quarter of 2009, Japan's output plummeted a record 14.2 percent, and the sixteen-country Euro currency zone saw a 10 percent retreat. U.S. housing prices dropped 31.4 percent. The Treasury Department spent $440 billion on automobile and bank stocks and $182 billion to bail out insurance giant AIG. A total of $144.5 billion was moved from stocks to treasury bonds, precipitating a huge drop in stocks worldwide. Unemployment rates remained above 9 percent till after 2010.

What made the 2008–09 financial crisis different from the other economic recessions before it was that this one created a worldwide liquidity issue. A little history first.

Mortgages are loans that are typically paid back over time, with the terms of the loan being renewed regularly, say every five years. The bank funds this loan with a deposit that has the same five-year term. So the loan is "match funded." If the borrower pays the loan off in fewer than five years, the bank is still obligated to pay the interest it agreed to on the deposit for the rest of the five years. Therefore, the person paying off the loan pays an interest penalty to enable the bank to meet its commitment to the depositor.

That's the system in Canada. But in the U.S., the system became different over time. In many U.S. states, customers could pre-pay the mortgages without paying an interest penalty. Of course, this made it impossible for the bank to put the loan on its balance sheet at the outset, in an effort to avoid the risk of having to continue to pay the depositor the contracted interest rate without receiving the corresponding contracted loan interest to fund the obligation.

So two things happen: 1. The bank sells the mortgage it has just originated to the market. 2. But it also loses the contact with the borrower in the process.

And so developed the U.S. the secondary market for mortgages (which persists to this day). Banks and other "originators" routinely sold the mortgages they had originated into the secondary market. Two large government-sponsored entities, known as Freddie Mac and Fannie Mae, were very significant participants in their secondary market. This has become a huge collection of loans that are effectively anonymous as to who and where the borrower is, which makes it very hard to follow up when the loan goes into arrears.

Thankfully, we have a different model in the Canadian banking system, where the vast majority of mortgages are done by people at the local branch in Truro or Trail who know the borrower. They're a retail customer of the bank, not some number in cyberspace. And we can fund it long-term by issuing a certificate of deposit on it. In the Canadian banking system, you maintain contact with the borrower.

In contrast, in the U.S., there was this floating wholesale market run by the investment bankers on Wall Street, with no regard for one of the fundamental principles of business that I have long adhered to: just because you are allowed to do something doesn't mean it's the right thing to do.

At the same time, there was political pressure to expand home ownership. The preferred (and easy) way for politicians to accomplish this "socially beneficial" goal was to put pressure on mortgage grantors, banks and others to loosen up lending standards and criteria, and pressure the wholesale market to accept in their pools loans of lower quality.

Then it got worse, when the financial wizards who thought up these derivatives got credit rating agencies like Moody's or Standard & Poor's to give this mess a triple-A rating. But these products that were triple-A-rated weren't really triple-A quality. They were more like C-minus. These collateralized debt obligations in the U.S. housing market, and their financing, were a bubble of wholesale funding on an insecure product. At the first sign of a liquidity squeeze, it all began to collapse, taking down the very financiers who were in the business of doing this, starting with Lehman Brothers. That cascaded into the whole financial system, because there's an interlocking of wholesale lending practices between banks to fund each other. It got very scary, very fast. Author Michael Lewis does a masterful job describing this process in his wonderful book, *The Big Short*.

While it originated in America, the crash had severe repercussions in Canada. Luckily, the Canadian economy entered the recession later than most other Western economies and was protected from the wildest of the real estate practices that sank the U.S. But the systemic problems were still felt across the whole banking industry. Now it's not just their problem; it's *all* of ours — we're in this together. You immediately had the Bank of Canada, the government and the heads of the banks all saying we've got a real serious problem here, what are we going to do?

Although they said they hated to do it, the U.S. federal reserve and American banks provided liquidities. They poured more money into the system to get over this liquidity problem. The Canadian economy could not distance itself from the imminent collapse of industries such as the auto industry, for instance. So we were obliged to provide large amounts of stimulus into those industries to keep them solvent — and protect tens of thousands of jobs. It took CEOs working around the clock every day with the heads of the government and central banks to do this in 2008.

Bill Downe, our new CEO in 2007, was in these kinds of meetings to represent BMO. Talk about Johnny-on-the-spot. I had put Bill in charge of capital markets after he'd been running the U.S. businesses, and the capital markets guys were unsure: "How could you put a commercial banker in charge of an investment bank?" But Bill proved his mettle during the liquidity crisis. And BMO (with other Canadian banks) rebounded even as the American and global systems were still in turmoil.

Thanks to our prudence in Canada — and some leadership at the political level starting with Prime Minister Stephen Harper, finance minister Jim Flaherty, and Bank of Canada Governor Mark Carney — we managed to dodge the worst of the fallout from the crisis that shook people's faith in the financial system. To me it proved another classic example of the strength of our banking regulations and, in contrast, the danger of letting politicians get into the mortgage business — as happened in the U.S. when they liberalized lending laws. While I had just left the CEO post at BMO, I couldn't have been prouder of how we reacted in a time when quick thinking and cool heads were needed.

Now my successors are dealing with an even more insidious challenge — the COVID-19 pandemic — that has few, if any, precedents in recent memory for the banking system. The stress on the health and financial systems of the world is unprecedented. Old solutions no longer apply; creativity and flexibility are paramount. But I hope, as the ripples of this pandemic make their way around the world, that people of character and resolve emerge to guide us as they have in the past. As always, I remain a believer in our creativity and resolve.

TONY'S TAKEAWAY

When asked by a reporter in the 1960s what he most feared, British Prime Minister Harold MacMillan was reported to have said "Events, my dear boy. Events." Periods of crisis are inevitable in the tenure of any leader. Through all the pivotal crises I witnessed and weathered at BMO, I learned there is no substitute for good old-fashioned strategy — accompanied, one always hopes, by flawless execution if, and when, the next crisis unavoidably hits.

VOICE: JACK O'BRIEN, PART 3

I remember the time when Tony needed $200 for something and asked me if I was in a position to lend it to him. Which I was. But when I give it to him, he insisted on writing me a receipt.

"You're kidding me, right?" I said with not a little disdain. "I know you're good for it. And even if you aren't, losing 200 bucks isn't going to kill me."

"Ah, yes," he replied, "but what if I die? How are my folks going to know that I owe you money?"

"Who cares?"

"I do," he said with finality, and wrote me out a receipt.

This struck me at the time as overkill; in my estimation it was totally unnecessary. Seven years later, however, I told my new bride about the incident, and she just nodded. It made perfect sense to her way of thinking, and she was somewhat stunned that I could be so financially naïve: "Thank God guys like Tony and not guys like you got into banking," she said.

CHAPTER 20

Algorithms and Aristotle: Recipe for Success

People have managed to marry without arithmetic.
— GEOFFREY CHAUCER, *The Canterbury Tales*

I've talked about why we thought it important to instill learning at the Bank. But why is learning so important to me? How does it underpin everything that I've done in my career? And how did it apply, even in the commercial world? I mean, what's a banker doing mixing Aristotle and interest rates?

Allow me a personal digression in the midst of this book on my banking life. As experienced as I am in the worlds of finance and technology, I believe that success in business stems from more than spreadsheets and algorithms. Throughout my career at the Bank I always sought to answer problems analytically. Whether it was introducing computers or improving traditional banking, I felt there was a way to use logic and reasoning, the disciplines of the classics, to solve problems. I had studied the classics in school, but it was after joining the Bank that I came to understand their philosophies in the context of a modern world.

It turns out that just about everything we need to know about the fundamentals of doing good business can be learned from the ancient Greeks such as Aristotle. He embraced the inscription on the Apollo temple at Delphi, *Meden Agan*, or, the Golden Mean. This is a brilliant way of saying that all strengths are weaknesses and all weaknesses are strengths. For example, bravery is a very good thing, but when pushed to an extreme, it becomes recklessness. The Golden Mean, the *meden agan*, the middle way, became Aristotle's abiding philosophy. (That was a valuable guide to me when we faced challenges at the Bank, from the non-merger to the U.S. derivatives meltdown to embracing technology. Having the chutzpah to take risks and be at the cutting edge needs to be tempered with due diligence and a carefully considered way forward.)

I've said it before, but my motto at the Bank was always to do the thing that brings the most good and the greatest happiness to the most people. That's a philosophy of life rather than a business principle. In fact, my liberal arts education and my grounding in the classics always served me well in my working life, and they informed not only who I am as a person, but who I became as a leader. As important as formal education and training are to professional success, I have always appreciated the value of lifelong learning, learning for its own sake and the value of a curious mind.

Part of my interest in learning stems from my family history. My paternal grandfather, who died when I was two months old, was a great intellectual and a voracious reader. He was even inspired to convert to Catholicism because he was influenced by the great writers and thinkers who came out of the Oxford Movement. And my grandfather passed that love of learning on to my dad.

My father didn't have the opportunity to go to university for formal studies, because it was the Depression and he had to work. He always was sensitive about that as a result. But, like his own father, he was also a great reader and a great student. After working in the financial industry his entire adult life, my father went back to school in his late seventies, enrolling at York University to get his degree in history. I think he was eighty-two when he finally graduated. My mother went back to school too — to the Ontario College of Art — and graduated in 1978. Meanwhile, my brother has a PhD in psychology and my sister got a degree in nursing and was head of obstetrical nursing at St. Mike's. And all my cousins are high school teachers and principals. So the entire family has always embraced and prioritized learning.

In practical terms, my never-ending quest for learning is an effort to figure out what life is all about, and what we can do with this life to make a difference. I have been wrestling with that my entire life, as I have been with other things. And it always comes back to one phrase, a beautiful phrase, that goes back to Aristotle and was Liz's mantra and philosophy of life: One person can make a difference. It all comes down to having a purpose in life.

It really is as simple as that. So simple that I've got only three bookmarks in my computer. One is Google, one is Amazon and the other is the ancient Greeks' different words for love. Today we use that one word to describe a wide range of emotions, but, as John Alan Lee wrote in *The Colours of Love*, the Greeks had as many as six different words for love. They started off with *eros*, which is passionate, sexual love. And then there is *ludus*, which is kind of like playful, joyful love — maybe flirting or playing with the kids, this kind of stuff. And then they worked their way to something called *pragma*, which is the mature love that you see in longstanding marriages and relationships. It's an understanding, a way to compromise. It's a beautiful concept, because it transcends the *eros*, the fling, which a lot of people *think* is happiness. The "I'm in love, hearts and flowers" notion. There's nothing wrong with that, but it doesn't last. *Pragma* — the root of pragmatic — is the real love: that state that those in mature relationships come to where they appreciate the good in each other and understand the other's needs and likes and wants. And it includes compromise.

The last one, which is very important, is *philautia*. *Philautia* is self-love. Self-love, according to the Greeks, is not narcissism, staring in the pool and admiring yourself. Rather, it's having an appreciation of your strengths. With self-love comes self-knowledge and the ability to live an authentic life, living up to a certain set of values, which you adhere to irrespective of what others might think. *Philautia*, self-love, means that you don't live for what other people are going to say about you; you know yourself, love yourself and follow your purpose in life. *Philautia* is what drives me to do the things that I think are right, and I will continue to do those regardless of what others think and do. And I don't sit and mope because somebody's upset with me. If you don't love yourself, you can't love anybody else, and you have nothing to give. This Greek concept of self-love is what guided me to be an authentic leader, to conduct myself at work according to my principles and to be the type of manager who could give of himself to help and develop others.

To develop a fuller understanding of what I know of the great scholars going back to the Ancient Greeks and into the Middle Ages, I'm now taking medieval studies at U of T. Some would say, who gives a damn about Medieval Studies? I do, and that's why I instituted the Comper Professorship in Medieval Studies at St. Michael's College at the University of Toronto. My instructor, Dr. Alison More, a highly regarded Latinist whose research investigates the intersections of social and religious culture in late-medieval Northern Europe, is the first holder of the chair.

What I find fascinating about medieval studies is how much was almost lost. Too much is gone, destroyed by the barbarians and wars and other kinds of calamity. (The estimate is we have only 20 percent of the literature from the time.) Classics, sacred literature, art: all nearly gone. We owe a great debt of gratitude to the religious scholars of the Middle Ages because they were responsible for preserving and carrying forward the learnings of classical antiquity, which would otherwise have been lost forever.

Thomas Cahill talks about this is his 1995 book *How the Irish Saved Civilization*. It was the monks and the scholars, squirrelled away in their tiny huts and cloisters, who preserved the classic literature and brought it forward. We therefore owe them a great debt of gratitude, as we do to Jerome and Augustine, even Charlemagne, who was a genius. It was his chief of staff, a man by the name of Alcuin, an English scholar, clergyman, poet and teacher from York, who designed the whole educational system for the Middle Ages of the year 800 — the system that persists until today.

And then there was St. Thomas Aquinas, picking up from there, saying to Christians, "Guess what, this guy Aristotle was the best philosopher that we'll ever see." And so Aquinas wrote his commentaries on Aristotle, and squared the circle of how you can bring together reason and faith. That was Aquinas's great contribution. A brilliant guy who had once been a traditionalist. This, in an era when having the wrong opinion could get you excommunicated or burned as a heretic. We haven't seen his equal since.

I've also learned that we don't give as much credit to the role that women in medieval times played in the intellectual development of knowledge. It's like everything else: our impression of women is based on the history that's been written by those who won the wars, as Napoleon famously said about history. And the nuns who were some of the most prominent educated women of the time were always deemed to be subservient, making garments for the priest and the monks. But that truly undermines their real roles in the history of the times. These women were great scholars and intellectuals in their own right and, in fact, wrote a lot of the manuscripts. While St. Patrick ran the Church in the north of Ireland, St. Brigid was a dominant presence in the Catholic Church in southern Ireland in the fifth century. She was an abbess and founder of several monasteries of nuns, including that of Kildare. This significant contribution was something I thought a lot about as we tried to incorporate women into the executive of the Bank.

My interest in the great women in arts and learning has also made me passionate about art in Canada, and how the Bank can support it. Sarah Milroy, the chief curator now at the McMichael Canadian Art Collection in Kleinburg, Ontario, has organized a show called *Uninvited: Canadian Women Artists in the Modern Moment*, an exhibition of women artists from the 1920s and 1930s who were never included in the Group of Seven. These women were known as the Beaver Hall Group, after the area of Montreal on the mountain. It was always claimed that they were simply the daughters of wealthy Anglo businessmen in Montreal who just dabbled in art. And that is, if I may say this, complete rubbish. In many cases, they were better artists than the men, but they were rarely invited into the boys' club. Only some male artists like A.Y. Jackson gave them their due.

Sarah's show was in appreciation of the role these women played. She used three of my paintings to put in the show, and one was the centrepiece of the whole exhibit. Making that contribution towards mounting the show is my version of paying it forward. I have been so fortunate to have a rich education in the arts and the classics, learning more than I thought possible through them to guide me through my business career as well as my personal life. That intellectual training is the solid foundation on which my success at the Bank was built and that, in turn, gave me the privilege of wealth. But as Aristotle so widely observed, my fulfillment is not in acquiring wealth and material possessions, but rather in using that privilege to give back in any way I can.

TONY'S TAKEAWAY

The classics have taught me the importance of living my life with purpose and authenticity to bring happiness — all the versions of it — as much as possible and to as many people as possible in life. They taught me that one person can make a difference. Even in a bank.

VOICE: NANCY GRECO

Nancy Greco has been a valued colleague and partner in arms for more than two decades, first during my term as chairman and CEO of BMO, and then as a director of my two foundations after retirement (the FAST Foundation, and the Elizabeth and Tony Comper Foundation). A highly valued advisor who assists me with both personal and business activities, she is the face of the Bank to several clients of BMO that I supported in my tenure as CEO and now in my retirement.

I met Elizabeth Comper in October 1999 when I joined the office of the president and CEO at the Bank of Montreal and began working for Tony as his executive secretary. Elizabeth became my mentor and friend. I have countless memories of the many adventures I was lucky enough to experience with her, from dining at the most fabulous restaurants, shopping in the most exquisite boutiques, travelling to New York to visit Robert Stern Architects during the construction of their beautiful home, to travelling across the world to Shanghai to attend the BMO Annual General Meeting. In addition, there are many life lessons I carry in my heart always. During my tenure in the CEO's office, Elizabeth was behind the scenes every step of the way.

VOICE: **ENZO GRECO**

Enzo Greco joined me in my retirement as my project manager to aid in the management of my investments — in particular, my real-estate investment portfolio. He is a skilled administrator and a compassionate and effective property manager. In his spare time, he coaches, manages and plays on two hockey teams and a baseball team. He is a key player and highly valued advisor.

Tony's generous contributions have impacted the lives of many around him. I'm amazed at the size of his heart and the trusting nature he extends to others, always looking at the positive side in life. Tony hired me in 2014 as a project manager to coordinate all the varied aspects of his life in retirement. After twenty-five years as an event planner, I wasn't sure about this complete career change and, frankly, I was a bit nervous about the prospect. From managing a large number of staff to working out of someone's private home: it would be a big change, and this decision weighed heavily on my mind.

Nancy, my wife and Tony's executive assistant at BMO for over twenty years, suggested we go to dinner with Tony and have a conversation with him about the job and my future. Immediately, I knew my transition was the correct route to take as Tony's proposal was very convincing. At dinner, Tony was kind, thoughtful and spoke with such clarity regarding my new job, it didn't take much afterthought to accept this new position.

Working daily with Tony is a true delight, as we discuss the current needs of his home, the needs of his newly constructed office and, most importantly, the needs of his true joy, Tessa, a four-pound, eight-year-old Shih Tzu/Bichon Yorkie — a benefit of the job I did not expect to manage.

As I observe him dealing with financial colleagues, cultural centres and all his foundation work, I have come to learn that this man has one true dominant gene, and that is generosity. Combined with that is his ever-present respect for others, respect for his former colleagues and respect for life in general. And that comes back to him in spades. Not a dinner meeting or sporting event goes by without someone approaching Tony just to shake his hand and say hello.

Our friendship continues to grow. I'm always impressed when Tony introduces me as his colleague and not his staff. Although some may think that trivial, I find it very genuine and respectful, characteristics that are deeply ingrained in Tony. I look forward to new adventures, new projects and new challenges with Tony, and I know that with him as my boss and mentor, our future is nothing but bright!

CHAPTER 21

BMO History:
In the Footsteps of Greatness

Life is short. Art long. Opportunity is fleeting. Expierience treacherous. Judgement difficult.
— GEOFFREY CHAUCER, *The Canterbury Tales*

To me, the history of the Bank of Montreal informs everything I've done or experienced at the Bank. As I walk through the doors of any BMO building, I have always been acutely aware of the legacy of those who went before me — from the founders to the senior managers I worked for and learned from to the mentors I was lucky to have as I worked my way through the ranks and into executive leadership positions. I felt the weighty responsibility to be a worthy steward of the impressive institution they built and nurtured.

There are probably few people who would have had my penchant for going back and finding out why over 200 years ago a group of Montreal businesspeople, including John Molson, Peter McGill, Augustin Cuvillier, two Americans and others decided that forming the Bank of Montreal was a good thing to do. That was a long time ago, and the country was a different place, but they lived in a market economy, just as we do today, and the same need for financing existed then to fund the burgeoning enterprises and economy of what would become Canada.

The Bank's past exists in a funny kind of a compression in my mind. The history that has unfolded since 1817 is not old photos and stories of distant memories to me; it's more contemporaneous in my mind. I don't know why. It doesn't feel like history as I walk through the head office building in Montreal. I've always loved it, so I've kind of lived the Bank's heritage over my forty years there. For example, I can almost tell you chapter and verse what happened in 1906 when the Bank of Montreal rescued the Ontario Bank from financial difficulty and absorbed its operations. Or when the Bank made the commitment to help build the Canadian Pacific Railway to bind the nation.

The premise for the founding of the Bank, as you can read from its early history, was the perceived need for homegrown financial support for Canadian enterprise at the time. (Hence the railway funding later that century.) Until then, it had all been coming from Britain or the United States. And so there was an incipient need for a domestic bank that could finance the growing and emerging market of Canada. Without local financing, we were simply going to be a branch-plant economy continuing to rely on funding from Britain or America.

The founders were all successful, savvy businessmen living in a new land of hope and prosperity. They came to the party as not just any merchant down the street but as prominent figures in the Montreal community and beyond. Horatio Gates, for instance, one of our two American regional shareholders was, at the beginning, instrumental in opening the flour market in the West. They all knew their way around business in Montreal and the emerging nation. Even in those days there was some pretty stiff competition, and they could relate to the need for local financial support not just for their own businesses but also for other new enterprises essential to building and growing the economy of the New World.

I don't think the founders thought there was anything profound about the establishment of the Bank. I don't imagine they set out to create what would, two hundred years later, be seen as one of the biggest and most successful corporations in the country; I think they simply had a common understanding of Canada as a young and growing nation (it wasn't even called Canada at the time). If it was going to continue to grow and develop, there was a huge demand and need for ongoing local financing for the enterprises that would be the backbone of the emerging economy. For instance, one of those needs was to finance the building of the Lachine Canal, which would allow boats to avoid the deadly rapids that stopped transport near Montreal.

Naturally, in the Bank's long and storied past it has seen many ups and downs. Even before we got our incorporation there were bumps on the road. The Bank had to withstand the uncertainty brought on by rebellions in both Upper and Lower Canada in 1837. Then there were the threats from America, which still coveted the territory to the north. But through all the economic cycles in its over two hundred years it has been a paragon of prosperity and stability. Only twice did the Bank of Montreal fail to declare a dividend, in 1827 and 1828. Since then, they have paid a dividend every single year — even through the Great Depression of the 1930s. One economic historian has said that if the banks hadn't been intentionally constructed the way they were, they would have all gone under completely in the period of the Great Depression, when they were technically bankrupt.

The early days of the Bank were also full of interesting characters, as well as some business deals that we would never see today. In the 1860s, for example, there was a huge economic downturn, primarily in Ontario. Around this same time, the Bank determined in their wisdom that there was an opportunity to invest and trade in gold on the New York market. So we used all of our resources, and we almost cornered the gold market in New York. Almost, but not quite.

One of the directors of the Bank at the time was William McMaster. He lived in Toronto and would take the train to Montreal for board meetings, as train travel was customary in those days. It was alleged that the Bank had made some investments at the expense of calling in a number of loans in Ontario, causing financial distress to many customers there. McMaster, who was a good Torontonian, took great umbrage at this.

He noisily left our board, turning his back on the Montreal business connections and focusing on interests in the city of Toronto, where he became very busy. Among the organizations he founded was the Canadian Bank of Commerce (forerunner to today's CIBC), which opened for business in 1867 with McMaster as its first president. In 1881 he was instrumental in creating the Toronto Baptist College on Bloor Street in the building that is now the Royal Conservatory of Music. The College eventually became an independent university in 1887 and was named McMaster University to honour the large bequest left to the school upon his death in 1888 (the college moved to Hamilton, Ontario, in 1930). One wonders if McMaster would have gone on to establish all these venerable institutions — and one of BMO's major competitors — if the Bank of Montreal had not called in some loans in Ontario while he was a director. I love those kinds of stories.

With all these challenges, it's fair to ask why did the Bank of Montreal survive when some of the others of the day didn't? There were many competitors that fell early on. From 1890 to 1920 there was a period of consolidation in the banking business, whether it was the Exchange Bank of Yarmouth in 1903, the People's Bank of Halifax in 1905 or the People's Bank of New Brunswick in 1906. They would typically face problems, because they didn't have a diversified loan portfolio. One business segment or one industry or one geographical region would fail and the whole loan book would go and the bank would be in trouble. As mentioned in Chapter 16, that's what happened to the Newfoundland banking system in the 1890s, long before it became a Canadian province in 1947. The Bank of Montreal helped rescue it by investing considerable sums of money to prop up the economy, and to this day BMO still has a large presence in the province as a result. Diversification was a key to the Bank of Montreal's survival in the early days, as it was for the nation's banking system at the time, and it remains so to this day.

Most people today wouldn't know what Polk's Directory was, but it was like a big telephone directory for businesspeople. (There were versions in many cities over the years, and this was how you had to look up information before the advent of the internet.) With Polk's, you paid money, and you got an advertisement in their book. I once saw an advertisement that the Bank had run in the London, England, version of Polk's Directory in 1864, which boasted: "Paid up capital 130,000 pounds sterling." That was a lot of money in those days — and worth bragging about. The ad then listed all the branches of the Bank of Montreal and each branch manager's name in Canada — a testament that the Bank of Montreal was already a formidable institution operating on the world stage.

So, when I was feeling a little mischievous, my skill-testing question to our bankers was always, "Where were those branches in 1864, and who were the branch managers?" Of course, the second part of the question about branch managers in 1864 is impossible to answer. But what about the first question? Where were the branches in those days? No one can answer that precisely either — two were in the province of Quebec. Bank No. 1 was in Quebec City. Bank No. 2 was in Montreal. Next there were twenty-four branches in Southern and Central Ontario, including: Kingston, Ottawa, Cornwall, Whitby, Toronto, London, Arnprior, Smiths Falls, Peterborough. All close to Lake Ontario and the Rideau Canal, the primary transportation systems of the day. And then the branches headed to the east in the 1850s, throughout the Maritimes and into Newfoundland, after, as noted earlier, we, along with others, took over their banking system when it went broke in 1894.

Even in the early years, despite our name and the public perception, we weren't just about Montreal. We were always a Quebec and Southern Ontario bank, almost from the beginning. That was partly because of the transportation system, but also that's where the economy was in the day. The Ontario economy, at that time, was already significantly bigger than the Quebec economy. And why? More people lived there. And the Canadian brand became increasingly important as we started to go west when new provinces came on board. So then we were in Winnipeg, Calgary, Vancouver, Victoria. And then the Bank added fill-ins when the railway came in: Rosetown, Castlegar, Trail, Golden.

The Bank of Montreal was heavily involved in raising capital in London, England, and in the United States for financing the transcontinental Canadian Pacific Railway. The massive project was deemed near impossible. It's not as though they give you a detailed plan of how they're going to put a railway through Kicking Horse Pass in the Rockies with a grade so steep it boggles the imagination. Sometimes I try to think what it was like for the men at the Bank who made the decisions to go ahead with building the railway in the 1880s, one of the most ambitious projects ever undertaken in our country and an incredible feat of engineering. The beauty of history is imagining what it might have been like, how they could have even comprehended the task before them back in the day.

When I imagine the historic discussions that were going on in those board meetings, I can picture some bewildered director asking, "What the . . . do you mean we're going to put another 100 million pounds into this thing? Is it ever going to work?" I am convinced the bank believed the biggest thing in their favour was the commitment of Prime Minister Sir John A. MacDonald and the entire government to getting the CPR built. It was going to happen come hell or high water. It would never go bankrupt, and it would get bailed out if necessary — not unlike the way the Trans Mountain Pipeline was bailed out in 2018. When the government sticks its neck out, that's something you can probably hang your hat on.

The expansion of the railway also meant the expansion of the Bank of Montreal into Western Canada. Trains back in those days were powered by steam engines, which could go only about fifty miles or so before they had to tank up with water. There had to be a depot with a water tank every fifty miles, and since the Bank of Montreal was financing the railway, we were there at every stop.

Here's an interesting story about the "instant branches" that popped up along the railway line: The Bank had a flatbed car on a westbound train with a bunch of lumber on it. At every stop they'd push the lumber off and hammer it together to erect a building in no time flat. They could put up one of these instant branches across the West in just twenty-four hours, extending our presence right across the country. Gordon Lightfoot had it right in his "Canadian Railroad Trilogy": "They saw an iron road runnin' from sea to the sea."

Another of my favourite CPR stories is about the final push to get the railway through the Rockies in B.C. and how they figured out the route through the Gold Range of the Monashee Mountains near Revelstoke. This part of the railway was the final section of the CPR to be completed before the last spike was driven at Craigellachie, B.C., on November 7, 1885. The Scottish engineer Walter Moberly had reached a stalemate there. He couldn't figure out where the route should go next. There were many routes into the mountains that led nowhere. With the costs already so high, they couldn't spend money to just go forward on their best guess and then have to pull back and start over if it didn't work. The story goes that one day Moberly was standing looking at this perplexing landscape and wondering where to go next with his tracks.

As he stood there, he saw eagles flying through a cleft in the mountains. He turned to the scouts and said, "Let's follow the eagles, because they will know the way through the mountains." And so they did. That's why it's called Eagle Pass.

The railroad, for all its financial and political trouble to the Bank, was how we established our presence in the West and our branches soon spread across the country more widely than any other bank's, serving all those different communities with their own unique needs, helping them to survive and grow in locations like Wetaskiwin or Linden in Alberta. The homesteaders were there because, back in the early part of the twentieth century, the Canadian government would give you a section of land if you agreed to homestead it for three years. If you could do that then you got to keep it. (A surprising number couldn't meet the challenge.) That's how these farms got into the hands of individuals like my maternal grandfather, Hippolyte Dubé, in Saskatchewan.

The career model became a young man of, say, seventeen years of age who faced a choice: he could either work on the family farm or go into the business world. If the young fellow, just out of high school, decided he wanted to go into business, Dad went into town to talk to the local bank manager at Bank of Montreal. If the manager liked the young man, he would join the Bank. Then he would start to get moved from town to town. Every eighteen months or so — if he was smart, showed promise and was good at his job — he would get moved to another branch and a new community, to learn the business of banking on the job and gain experience in different communities.

Because he came from the West, he likely had a good understanding of the local farming communities, which were then a pervasive mix of a lot of our operations across the country. And so, our staff came by their knowledge of how those communities operated and the economics of local farming, the suppliers and equipment companies and things of that nature. As they wound up becoming the branch managers, they'd know half the people in the community and relate to them. All these managers had a unique knowledge of the towns, neighbourhoods and regions in which they worked. I'm using the example of Western Canada, but it was the same for young, aspiring employees across the country, including me. Back in the 1960s when I joined the Bank of Montreal, the whole model of development for junior bankers was having them learn on the job. That model influenced me and how I learned the business, just as it did for so many young people when Canada was still largely a rural, agrarian nation rather than an industrial, urban economy.

Now I have this other theory too. It's probably based on an apocryphal assumption, but it's a wonderful theory. These young men would start in these small towns (and the branch managers were all men then), and then eighteen months later they'd get transferred to a place like Moose Jaw. Their whole social life was with whom? With the branch people. Who were the branch people? Women — 70 percent of them. So their whole social life was with young women in different branches, and more often than not, they would develop a romantic relationship with one of the women in one of the branches, and they'd get married. I actually estimated at one point in time that 37 percent of employees at the Bank were related to one another. You can see my niece Katie working today at the Bay and Bloor branch in Toronto. And you'd see couples and then their daughters and sons working in the organization, generations of banking families. And some people would say, "Don't you think it's favouritism to hire family members into the Bank?"

I would say, "No, it's the best of all possibilities."

"Why?"

I always used the example of our head of bank services, a guy with a big job. Both of his daughters worked for BMO. His wife worked for BMO. "If his kids are working for the Bank, and those kids step out of line for three seconds, they're going to get snapped back into line so fast. There's no way that Mom and Dad are going to tolerate any poor performance from their kids because it reflects on them." To me, the family ties are a guaranteed way to keep a tight ship.

Here's another example of the family environment at the Bank: As I mentioned earlier in Chapter 4, I had joined the computer training program, which created IT professionals to automate the branch system, test it and build the programs. When I became VP of systems, I made a rule that we were going to keep the programming school that had trained me and many others open. Why? We pumped about fifteen to twenty new kids through the computer programmer training school every six months. You'd support one another in the challenges of the training and later on the job; you'd go out to lunch together and socialize. Your classmates were not only your colleagues — they became your buddies.

When the next version of the class graduated, the same thing happened. What was the result of these tightknit friendships developing? The rate of turnover in the application programming department was 5 to 6 percent, where the rate in the rest of the other industry IT shops was 15 to 20 percent. Why? Camaraderie. These program graduates associated with each other and they were close. Some met their future spouses at the Bank.

I even felt that some customers had a sort of family connection to the Bank when I transferred to England to become manager at our branch in central London, not terribly far from where our long-time branch at Waterloo Place had been. For Canadians travelling or working in London, having our bank there was a touch of home. And that original Bank of Montreal branch on Waterloo Place was burned into the memory of a lot of Canadian veterans. We were the only branch of a Canadian bank in London, England, at the time of World War II. So all the Canadian soldiers either had their bank account there or came in to have their money transferred to Canada. We became the bank of the Canadian Army. That is now in the long-ago past, forgotten for the most part. (By the way, after the war, we also served as the bank for the Canadian Army when they had two bases in Germany.)

Speaking of Europe and the two World Wars, there are all sorts of interesting historical documents in the vaults of the Bank about our foreign funding during wartime. What would you do if you had a collection bill that had to go into Holland or France during the fighting in WWI or WWII? Business still had to go on, right? We actually had forms called "trading with the enemy." There was a whole procedure developed, a whole machinery created to facilitate trade with Europe at a time when the Brits got into a European war. We needed to assure our supply of foreign funding would not dry up.

Or what happened when the Americans got into a civil war? There was a story there too, because we had a branch in Chicago prior to the American Civil War. We still have many documents in the BMO archives giving guidance to our branch in Chicago on how you continue trading quite delicately in the U.S. at the time of the Civil War. I love to browse those records when I get the time to visit the archives.

When the Great Chicago Fire happened in 1871, killing approximately 300 people and leaving more than 100,000 residents homeless, Bank of Montreal was the first financial institution to re-open its doors just after the disaster, responding to the needs of the local clientele. The interesting thing about Chicago in those days was that it was almost a freer trade model than New York, given that it was the epicentre of the emergent rail network in the U.S. So it was long an important city to the Bank, even before we bought the Harris Bank in 1984.

This being Canada, the Bank was also involved in hockey. The bank hockey league in Quebec and Ontario from the 1930s on was almost bigger than the NHL. The banks all had their own hockey teams, and it was a big thing for the employees. We would recruit all these terrific hockey players and put them on the payroll as a teller in the local downtown branch. A lot of them turned out to be really good bankers. Like Dave Neville, who ran one of our big branches and was the star centre for the Bank of Montreal's hockey team. He was hired as a hockey player and became a banker. It worked out that way for a few of them.

So, yes, it's a cliché for a big corporation to sometimes talk about "family" values. But knowing the history of BMO from its origins — some of it repeated here, I can use the term "family" unreservedly to describe the camaraderie we felt working there. And that might be the best epitaph you can offer for any business.

TONY'S TAKEAWAY

Learning from the Bank's past increases your appreciation of its current role in society and lets customers understand the value in its dependability. Whether it's learning about hockey players in the Bank's colours or sodbusters opening up banking on the Prairies, discovering the past has always increased my appreciation of the Bank's current place in the economic health of the country. These stories and many others are all part of the history that I carried with me every day after I made the decision to cast my lot in with Bank of Montreal. And I never regretted a day of that commitment.

CHAPTER 22

Matt Barrett: He Will Still Be the Indomitable Irishry

He bore himself so well in peace and war.
That there was no one Theseus valued more.
— GEOFFREY CHAUCER, *The Canterbury Tales*

From the first day I met Matthew Barrett when I flew to Montreal for my orientation at head office in December of 1970, we became very fast friends. He took me out for beers at a local pub, and our friendship naturally flowed from there. We became so close, in fact, that the following year when my wife-to-be, Liz, came to Montreal, she and I lived in Matt's apartment with Matt and Irene, his wife at that time, for the whole summer. I even became godfather to one of his daughters. Little did either of us dream in those early days that he would eventually end up as CEO of the Bank, and I would be his second-in-command before succeeding him as CEO myself.

He was then exactly the same as he has been all along: an absolute prankster. I'll tell you one stunt from our early days in Montreal. It was funny, because as recruitment coordinator, I would receive thousands of letters from hopefuls looking for a position with the Bank. They came from all over the world. One time, Matt was in cahoots with my secretary and he faked a letter. Pat, my secretary, came running in and she said, "Tony, it's about a Mr. So-and-So, and he is here in Montreal. He's come a long way from his home country and he's very excited about the job that you've offered him." She showed me a carbon copy of the letter that I had allegedly signed but that she had actually faked in concert with Matt.

I was so busy that I could easily have signed this stupid letter offering the poor guy a job. Then she said, "He's on the phone." And I get on the phone and, of course, it's Matt disguising his voice, calling himself "your humble servant" and going through an elaborate ritual about how he's so delighted, he's brought his entire family to Montreal for this job. And I'm thinking, *Who is this guy, and where will I be working next when word of this leaks out?* Just as I'm about to blow a fuse, Matt comes into the office. Tears are coming out of his eyes because he's laughing so hard. He had cooked up this whole scheme with my secretary. He had a wicked sense of humour. I can laugh about it now.

But I gave as good as I got, by the way.

I think I've told this story to only a few people. We had the two hundredth anniversary celebration in Montreal for the Bank in October 2017. There was to be a big unveiling of the wonderful display of the Bank's history, which had been set up in the main hall. And then there would be speeches by a variety of speakers, including me. Let me set the scene: the head office in Montreal is a beautiful old domed building, dating back to 1847. In 1890, architect Stanford White from New York was hired to design the addition behind the original building. In the corridor connecting the old building to the newer one, there is a sort of hall of memories. On the wall is a complete list of the Bank's previous management, all the names of the people who contributed over the years. The technology is amazing, because they actually drilled holes in the limestone to put in little brass letters for every single name. This is also where you can find James Earle Fraser's statue of *Victory*, dedicated to all the employees who died in World War I and II. And this is where they had installed this beautiful exhibit of the history of the Bank for the anniversary.

Of course, there was a crowd in attendance for the unveiling: staff, customers and all the dignitaries. After the formalities, a smaller group went up to the fourteenth floor for dinner. Rob Prichard had assiduously written to all the after-dinner speakers, telling each of us that we had three minutes speaking time — maximum.

Matt was scheduled to be the penultimate speaker, followed by me. Matt staying within three minutes? Forget it. He spoke for about fifteen minutes nonstop, as only Matt can do. And of course it was brilliant. I knew he would be, as always, so I had rehearsed carefully what I would say and how I would top his oration.

When Matt finally concluded, I got up and began, "The Lord has given each of us many crosses to bear." People were probably thinking, "Oh geez, Tony's going off-script . . . he's going rogue." I continued. "Mine is always to be the follow-up speaker to Matt Barrett . . ." The place broke up. Because they knew exactly what he was like.

Matt and I had a very close working relationship. When we'd embark on a plan he always gave me far more credit than I deserved for having examined all eighteen ways of why this project could go wrong, how it could get screwed up, how the directors could object. But then of course you'd walk into the boardroom and Matt would lecture the board on why this was the right thing. He'd head all their objections off at the pass, because we would have anticipated them and worked through them in advance. I was the catastrophizer and he was a great salesman, so we made the perfect team.

To paraphrase the old EF Hutton slogan, when Matt talked, people listened. He was knowledgeable in many areas, confident, eloquent and persuasive. From the board perspective, there was only one sales pitch that mattered, and that was the one from me and Matt. As long as I convinced Matt that something was a good idea or initiative, that was enough to get it done.

"Fine, if you're happy, I'm happy," he'd say. He trusted me implicitly to do the work that needed to be done, to consider every decision from all angles and to do the right thing. It was always an easy sale. "Tony," he often told me, "you run the Bank."

We'd both come up under Bill Mulholland. Bill was a tough WWII veteran who had joined the Bank in 1969–70 under tragic circumstances. He had been with Morgan Stanley in New York, and they were doing all the bond financing for the huge Churchill Falls Generating Station in Labrador. The top three executives of the British Newfoundland Development Corporation (BRINCO), the consortium developing this massive hydroelectric project, were killed in a private plane crash. Mulholland had been the financier, so he was named to become the new CEO of BRINCO. Their deceased CEO had been on our board, so Mulholland naturally took his seat on the Bank of Montreal's board. Then, in another twist of fate, the chap who was going to be our next chair, Len Walker, was diagnosed with cancer and died quite suddenly, in a matter of months.

So Arnold Hart, our president and CEO from 1959–70, temporarily wheeled himself back in from being a non-executive chair to run the place. He engaged with Mulholland and encouraged him to join the Bank as a full-time executive, not just as a director. So, Mulholland became president and chief operating officer, but not CEO, in 1975. He eventually assumed the role of CEO as well in 1980 and took over completely. He was unique. He came from out of left field a little bit, as he had come to us from outside the usual Bank channels. But he understood the need to modernize the Bank. He helped negotiate the acquisition of Nesbitt, Thomson and Company (later Nesbitt Burns Inc.) in 1987, which was the one of the first bank takeovers of a Bay Street brokerage. He was also a big fan of raising horses. He built Windswept Farm in Georgetown, Ontario, one of the world's leading stud farms for Hanoverian horses. It was his love of show-jumping that led to our sponsorship of the world-class equestrian facility at Spruce Meadows in Calgary.

He was a great role model for us. Mulholland gave way to Matt Barrett in 1989. I'd always known that Matt was the golden-haired boy as we moved up through the ranks. He was always two standard deviations ahead of me wherever he was going, and I was just putting my head down and doing whatever I was doing at the time inside the Bank. Matt was moving in other circles, but we got it done together. You'd be amazed at the latitude and authority he gave me and how much he would delegate to me.

Matt was not afraid of change and he was masterful in bringing everyone else along with him. Case in point, while focusing on the external business and rebranding the Bank's corporate image, he completely reformed the internal governance of the Bank. Back in 1974, there were, I believe, fifty directors of the Bank of Montreal. There was representation from all the regions of the country and a lot of other people. There was a very organized approach to governance in those days because there had to be. If you've got fifty people in a board meeting, you'd better conduct it in a very organized way or it will become pure chaos.

While governance of a major Canadian corporation with that many shareholders might have been right once, it was certainly outdated by the time Matt and I took over. There were still thirty-five directors at the Bank when we took the reins in 1989-90, and we would have an executive committee meeting in the middle of the month, and a board meeting at the end of the month. So there were twelve board meetings and twelve executive committee meetings a year — twenty-four meetings every year. I once totted up the number of board meetings that I had attended in ten years as chief operating officer and then ten years as CEO: 194 meetings. And not all of them were the most fascinating or interesting things that you could imagine, because there was a lot of routine business.

Matt realized that to manage a fast-moving company effectively in this day and age, we had to be more flexible. And that meant that we had to have a less bulky governance structure and become much more stream-lined. Gradually, over a period of about ten years, Matt managed the board down to about fifteen or sixteen people. You don't want to handle anything that important in a manner that is preemptive or too fast.

As careful and strategic as he could be as a leader, Matt would also take a much more humorous approach to some things, and he never hesitated to use very colourful language to describe the situations that he was sent in to clean up. I, meanwhile, the catastrophizer, would approach everything with eyes wide open, thinking, "This is a disaster, it's really bad. How much worse can it get?" We had two completely different approaches that were perfectly complementary.

He would always treat things with his indomitable Irish wit, even in the worst of circumstances. Sometimes that led to funny situations. We had a branch in downtown Montreal in the Alexis Nihon shopping centre opposite the old Montreal Forum. In the late 1970s, the branch was in trouble, so they sent Matt in to clean it up. He was like me, a problem-solver and a "cleaner upper" by profession.

After long days at work trying to clean up the business of that branch, we sometimes wound up hanging out at the bar nearby. There was a bongo player who performed there, and Matt, who was fairly knowl-edgeable about music himself, loved the guy. He would describe to me the bongo player's technique, and every once in a while, the performer would invite Matt up to play the bongos. And he was pretty good too.

While we were there, Matt taught me about Frank Sinatra. I didn't appreciate Sinatra then, and he schooled me on him: "Tony, Sinatra is a genius at phrasing the song."

"What do you mean by *phrasing*, Matt?" I asked.

Then Matt described to me what phrasing was and how Sinatra had learned how to breathe while he sang from watching Tommy Dorsey play the trombone. Dorsey could go eight, ten, twelve bars without taking a breath. So I started listening to Sinatra and I began to under-stand what Matt was talking about, which I thought was a brilliant insight. In fact, his dad had been a band leader, and even though Matt couldn't carry a tune or play an instrument, he was musically inclined and knowledgeable.

Matt's father had his band when he was back in County Kerry, Ireland, and there hadn't been a lot of money in the family. At the urging of his father, Matt went straight from high school in Ireland to the London office of Bank of Montreal as a clerk in 1962. Then he moved from London to Canada in 1967. Without any formal post-secondary education himself, he'd gotten by on his instincts and his charm to get ahead.

But Mulholland decided in 1981 that we were going to send Matt off to the Harvard advanced management program in Boston. He had a good time, and, I'm told, even showed up to class every once in a while. Harvard was very much into the case-study method at the time. And I remember Matt telling me, "Tony, the most profound thing, very early in the program, was when we had to solve a problem with our team. We had to go away and commit all the money they gave us for the exercise, grinding the numbers and come back into the classes.

"They asked us 'So what's your solution?' This guy I was working with does one of these problems they assigned us. We go through the numbers, and first of all, he's really deficient in his operating leverage. Number two, he's got to concentrate to get these expenses down." And,

Matt said, "I realized his approach was dead wrong. When somebody comes to you with a big pitch based on a detailed analysis with all these impressive numbers, what you have to do is ask yourself just one question: 'What is this guy really trying to accomplish?' Because his numbers will be focused on accomplishing what *he* wants to get done, not necessarily the solution to the problem."

A final Matt story. After I'd moved into treasury operations in 1984, Matt did something for me. He decided that I deserved time off for good behaviour. That was when he sent me to London, England — the locus for all of our business overseas — to run our international operations in the heart of global commerce for two years.

By seeing to that promotion, Matt was instrumental in helping to develop me as a leader and in grooming me for the executive track. He always emphasized the importance of training and development in the Bank. The culmination of that was, of course, the BMO Institute for Learning, which I explained in Chapter 11. I believe that his commitment to formal education for our staff grew out of his own upbringing, having to start at the bottom and work his way up by learning on the job. It is one of my proudest accomplishments that the legacy of learning and leadership that Matt Barrett and I started has been continued by Bill Downe and Darryl White and remains a high priority for the Bank to this day.

TONY'S TAKEAWAY

Matt Barrett was a charismatic leader who could walk into a room and light it up like a Christmas tree. Still, corporate success is rarely the product of a single personality. It takes a blend of backgrounds and experience and knowing how to manage that dynamic. Our complementary styles and personalities made us a great team and allowed us to accomplish many important things over our years together at BMO. My collaboration with this brilliant, funny, demanding and gregarious Irishman was the single most significant relationship of my professional career.

CHAPTER 23

The FAST Foundation: One Person Makes a Difference

Youth may outrun the old, but not outwit.
— GEOFFREY CHAUCER, *The Canterbury Tales*

During 2003 and 2004, Liz had been seeing reports on television about a number of anti-Semitic incidents in Toronto and Montreal. People were kicking over tombstones and painting swastikas on garage doors. In one report, they were interviewing a couple of young Jewish boys, maybe ten or eleven years old, who were terrified that this was occurring. They knew the history. As a society, we may have thought we had passed by all that sort of thing, but obviously the reality was very different for those in the Jewish community in Canada.

Liz corralled me one morning as I was shaving, and after reflecting on what she'd seen on TV the night before, she said, "Tony, we've got to do something about this." I wholeheartedly agreed and promised to think about what we might be able to do to counteract these kinds of hate crimes.

We got talking to Monte Kwinter, who was a Liberal cabinet member in the Ontario government of Dalton McGuinty in those days. He suggested doing something like Crime Stoppers. A very good thought, but this wasn't just about the criminal acts of hate themselves; there was much more behind the issue than that. Liz had been a teacher, so she strongly believed in education as a way of accomplishing change. Her philosophy, which was quite correct, was that all this prejudice was handed down in families — it's the intrafamilial transmission of hate, of deeply held biases against others who are different. That's how kids pick up hate, anti-Semitism, prejudice of any kind. It was clear to us, and to Liz in particular, that we had to tackle the problem through education, not prosecution. This was how FAST (Fighting Antisemitism Together) was conceived.

Liz also believed, as I do, that one person can make a difference. As a result, we got chatting with our friends Joe and Sandy Rotman and a few other people. Joe was very helpful, and if it was going to be an educational initiative, then he was on board with that. Joe was so committed to education that he was the principal benefactor of the Joseph L. Rotman School of Management at U of T. We were all on board with developing an educational program to make a difference in the lives of young people.

If you know anything about Jean Piaget's theory of cognitive development and his theories of early childhood development, you'll know that his many studies revealed that children go through different stages. Their brains can't grasp abstract concepts until they hit maybe ten or eleven years of age. Piaget's famous test involved two beakers: one was tall and narrow and the other was shorter and fatter. He'd take water, pour water into the tall beaker, filling it, then do the same with the shorter, wider beaker and ask young children, which one has the more water in it? They would consistently choose the tall one, until they could understand the concept of conservation of quantity.

Liz said that around the age of ten or eleven is the critical moment in a child's development when they can begin to understand abstract concepts; therefore, to break the cycle of intrafamilial prejudice, you've got to teach racial tolerance in Grades 6, 7 and 8. When we eventually developed educational materials to be distributed into the school system to change young minds, these are the grades we targeted. The whole program was aimed at teachers, with lesson plans and resources to support the learning we were trying to impart to the kids. Of course, everything had to conform to the curriculum requirements of all the boards — public, Catholic, French, English — across Canada, and we wanted to produce only one version, so that took about a year to convince all the boards of education that this could work.

FAST now offers two programs for different age groups. *Choose Your Voice* is a series of lesson plans and documentation aimed at students aged eleven to fourteen in Grades 6, 7 and 8. The second is *Voices into Action*, a curriculum-based teaching resource for Grades 9 to 12 that is also used for adult education. When Liz and I were involved with developing the second program for high school kids, we became close friends of David Booth and Larry Swartz, both professors. David Booth (who passed away in 2018) was a world-famous professor on curriculum development for children at Ontario Institute for Studies in Education (OISE), which is part of the University of Toronto. Larry is a renowned teacher and literacy consultant at OISE. They worked with us to develop the new program in fourteen different segments for the high school kids. To do it, they recruited twelve university professors from OISE and elsewhere to write the different modules.

To date, fourteen years after the initial rollout, the FAST programs have now been delivered to 4.2 million young Canadians and 22,000 schools across the country. And they are growing still. It's also gratifying that FAST has been recognized, winning the Award of Excellence from the Canadian Race Relations Foundation in 2010 for *Choose Your Voice* and in 2016 for *Voices into Action*.

I can't believe the scope this initiative has achieved since that morning Liz cornered me in the bathroom. The new version that started in 2018 for high school kids has now been delivered to more than a million high school students and four universities who are teaching teachers-in-training. It has also been picked up by correctional services to give to prisoners, teaching them about intolerance and how to deal with it.

The new version has expanded beyond just anti-Semitism to include content on other types of prejudice and discrimination, including residential schools and the genocides in Rwanda, Armenia and Ukraine. Both programs are available online and feature video segments throughout.

To get more exposure for the important work FAST was doing, I approached my friend Larry Tanenbaum — through his Toronto Raptors connections — to ask his star player Kyle Lowry to introduce one of the sections on diversity in his Raptors uniform. And Irwin Cotler, also a good friend and former Minister of Justice and Attorney General of

Canada, did one of the discussions at the front end of the video on toler-ance, diversity and human rights. With the help and support of these and other well-known people, the program has continued to grow. Sadly, the need for it seems to have only expanded.

Liz, as in everything else she did, became very passionate about this cause, and she would be invited by Jewish organizations across the country to speak about the initiative that had all started with her. To prepare, she'd say, "Tony, you've got help me, I've got to give this speech to the UJA [United Jewish Appeal] in Montreal in a month from now." So I'd write up a very careful three-page outline of a speech. And she'd take it and edit it, scribble all over it and pick out three things she really liked. And then she'd do her speech. She was great at talking about this issue because she was so passionate about it.

The best talk she ever did was when they were having Holocaust Education Week, for which BMO was a big sponsor, in venues all over Toronto. One of the locations was St. Monica's church in north Toronto. (The funny thing was that I had gone to St. Monica's Catholic School until I was in Grade 2.) To introduce her presentation, she played a clip from "You've Got to Be Carefully Taught," a song from the soundtrack of the musical *South Pacific* that says you have to be taught how to hate. Hate doesn't come naturally. Liz was very creative with things like that. Of course, her point was that's why we have to focus on educating kids in Grades 6, 7 and 8 how *not* to hate, as the way to intervene, if we're going to make any progress whatsoever.

Now, with Liz gone, Nicole Miller has been hired as FAST's exec-utive director, and there are coordinators across the country. They work with school boards and with the teachers in terms of the problems we face in eliminating prejudice. Nicole has now become a popular speaker in Israel — she's even gone viral for her speeches. She loves it. She's been doing it for over a decade now, and it's her passion in life.

I have been committed from the very beginning to funding the FAST organization and its programs. To get everything started, it was important to me that this initiative be spearheaded by people outside the Jewish community, to model the tolerance for others that we were trying to teach. So I recruited thirty of my friends and all the CEOs at the banks. I'd make a phone call and tell them about the two things I wanted: a commitment of $10,000 each. Plus, I wanted them to lend their own name and the name of their company in one-page ads that were going to run saying that we non-Jews were not going to stand for anti-Semitism anymore.

It took me hardly any time to make the calls and get all of these influential people on board with the seed money and their personal commitment to the cause. Since then, I've been leading the funding challenge personally, to the tune of half a million dollars a year. Liz really took this issue on as her own and took it to heart. It was so gratifying when she was recognized with the Order of Canada.

It was around Christmas time 2009, and there was a phone call from someone from the chancery office at Rideau Hall. I took the call. "Mr. Comper, I'm calling on behalf of the secretary to the Order of Canada. Your name is going to be put forward to receive the Order." I was pleasantly surprised; when she first said who she was, I thought she was going to ask me for a recommendation, since I'd given many before.

Then she added, "And there's more — your wife's name is going to go forward simultaneously. I believe it's only the third time in the history of the Order since 1967, when we invented it, that a couple has simultaneously received it." She told me the official announcement would be released on New Year's Day, and that I wasn't to say anything in the meantime.

I was a little surprised, to say the least, although pleased and, most of all, very proud of Liz.

Time went by, then in November 2011 we got up early to fly to Ottawa for the ceremony at Rideau Hall and to stay for a couple of days at the Chateau Laurier. We got to invite half a dozen friends to come along for the presentation and the party afterwards in Rideau Hall. At the ceremony, all of us went up one by one to receive the Order. They give you a citation, and a big medal (which I've never worn; it's upstairs packed away for safety). David Johnston, Governor General at the time, pinned the award on each person. Hayley Wickenheiser was appointed Officer and Robert Lepage was appointed Companion (these two ranks are the top ranks of the Order) at the same ceremony. Liz and I were made Members of the Order of Canada.

The entire thing was lovely and the Governor General was very gracious. The dinner that followed the ceremony was black-tie and all very formal. All our guests were there and the whole evening was actually quite touching. Liz just loved it.

There is a special version of the medal for women, which is more like a brooch with a bow on it. The award most people see is the lapel pin, which I wear on my jacket daily — as required — with pride. They tell you no matter what other honours you may get, the Order of Canada pin has got to take the pride of place. You have to wear it all the time.

The main reason cited for our awards was our philanthropic work — primarily the FAST Foundation, which was still in its early days at that time. Of course they also went into my accomplishments in business and Liz's past involvement in the arts. So, it was a little Christmas tree of stuff with the capstone for both of us being the recognition of the FAST Foundation. To this day, I don't know who put us forward, but the entire experience was very rewarding, and I remain grateful for it, especially as validation for Liz and all the great work she had started. When she passed away in 2014, I collected all of her speeches and got noted author Rod McQueen to help edit them and put them into a book that we published. It was another tangible expression of all the amazing work she had achieved and the good she had done.

Building on the work we had done with FAST, Issy Sharp, founder of the Four Seasons hotel chain, recruited me for a special project. He was hoping to build a Jewish museum, and he wanted to use the site of the former McLaughlin Planetarium just north of Queen's Park in Toronto, which had been kind of hanging around unoccupied for years, and nobody knew what to do with it. Issy recruited me to be an advisor on this project, although I'm not Jewish and I know nothing about museums. But he was not concerned. My role was to speak confidentially with prominent people in the Jewish community about whether this was a good idea. I was simply to be the neutral listener, gathering up their feedback and facilitating the process.

Heather Reisman and Gerry Schwartz invited me around for brunch on a Sunday. I'd known both of them for years. I was there to get their opinion on the proposed Jewish museum, but then halfway through brunch, Gerry said to me, "Heather and I talked about this before you came over. We're going to give a million dollars to your FAST Foundation."

"Gerry," I protested, "I told you, I don't take any money from the Jewish community."

He just laughed and said, "Tony, that was like ten years ago and everybody knows how principled you've been about this from the beginning, so just take the money." And so I eventually did. They have become very generous supporters of FAST.

FAST is now an established, thriving organization with a life of its own, and I'm not getting any younger. One of these days, like everybody else, I'm going to die. Where does FAST go from here? *Quo vadis?* What's going to be next for the foundation that Liz and I started all those years ago? Thankfully, I've been able to conclude an agreement with Dr. Catherine Chatterley, founding director of the Canadian Institute for Studies in Antisemitism, to join forces in fighting antisemitism in the future. She is highly respected, and we share our mission to eliminate antisemitism and intolerance through education. I am optimistic that the good work of FAST will continue under her leadership. I owe that to Liz, to honour FAST as her great legacy.

TONY'S TAKEAWAY

One person's commitment to doing good can still move mountains. Liz was the proof.

VOICE: JUDY TANENBAUM

Judy Tanenbaum and her husband, Larry, have been dear friends of me and my wife Liz . Judy is a leader in supporting Jewish charitable organizations and causes and is a supporter of Israel. She is an intellectual and has been a key advisor in the development of our FAST program. En passant, Judy and Larry have raised a beautiful and remarkable family.

I remember the first time I met Tony. It was at a dinner for the Canadian Council of Christians and Jews, and the speaker was his wife, Elizabeth, who brought goodness and sunshine into every room. I knew that an extraordinary moment happened as I listened to what Tony and Elizabeth deeply cared about: people in the world around them, minorities who had genuine issues in Canada.

Tony is an activist scholar. He identifies a problem, he studies it in depth, and then in his sure-footed and powerful way, he creates a platform, hires the best people in the field and finds a way to make a difference — not a small difference, but one that moves the needle. Jews battling anti-Semitism were the beneficiaries of the Compers' vision in creating FAST — Fighting Antisemitism Together. Aged Chinese Canadians in need of extended geriatric care benefitted from the opening of the Yee Hong Centre for Geriatric Care, created for them to provide this help within their cultural comforts and traditions. Indigenous people in need of integration and support in the workplace found opportunity in programs developed by BMO. Victims of the scourge of bullying on social media were given support through *Choose Your Voice.*

Tony spearheaded all of these programs, and he stays with them, following the details and always looking to reach the next height. It is a gift to Larry and me to have shared a warm and loving friendship with Elizabeth and Tony. Although Elizabeth is now gone and greatly missed, her spirit and outstanding work alongside Tony live on for the genuine benefit of all whom she and Tony touched. Tony is a true giant in caring for his fellow man. Larry and I are blessed by, and will forever treasure, this friendship.

CHAPTER 24

Elizabeth's Tale

But Christ's lore and his apostles twelve,
He taught and first he followed it himself.
— GEOFFREY CHAUCER, *The Canterbury Tales*

O f all the collaborations in my life, the best and most rewarding one of all was with my wife, Liz. People may not believe it, but Liz and I never had a fight in forty-three years of marriage. She was very intelligent, very thoughtful, very . . . grounded. She could relate to everybody and make them feel comfortable, whether she was sitting with Judy Tanenbaum at the Air Canada Centre (as it was known then) or with the waitress in the clubhouse at the Devil's Paintbrush golf course (to whom Liz gave one of her beloved camellias). She had that human touch.

While I had my head down at the Bank, she was my connection with reality. She was plugged into everything that was going on in everyday life and had a very gentle way of talking about the other side of any issue that I disagreed on. She never said anything to me like, "That's stupid," but soon enough — *eureka!* — I would come to the conclusion that she was telling me that I was being an ass. Not in so many words, because I might have pushed back. She just quietly nudged me in that direction, showing me the other side of the coin.

She was hugely supportive of my career. I learned only after she was gone that she was very protective of me at the office too. When I recruited Nancy Greco to be my assistant, she was only twenty-nine years old, and I was CEO and chairman of the Bank. Nancy was very talented and intelligent, but she was inexperienced. She later told me that Liz would spend hours on the phone with her, advising her on who she should and shouldn't let in to see me, filling her in on who was a pain to deal with and so on. I didn't know any of this was going on until Liz had passed.

She was a trooper — even when she was ill in the last three years of her life. We had an extremely busy and demanding social life when I was an executive at BMO. Two or three nights a week, I'd tell Liz we had another function, or we had to have dinner with a client on Thursday. I knew it was tough on her, me dragging her to these things when she'd rather just stay home and relax. And I'd say, "Never again, this is the last one. I promise. But let's go. I'm never going to ask you to do this again." She knew it wouldn't be the last time, but she'd still go along with it. Then she'd walk into the dinner smiling. She exuded social grace and would genuinely enjoy herself until I had to drag her home at three o'clock in the morning, like she was the last one there. Everybody said, how come Liz is always so lovely and charming?

I thought she was charming the first day I met her in 1966. She had a friend who suggested she come to the Delta Tau Delta fraternity at U of T to see my band, that I had named The Compleat Works. I guess my long hair didn't bother her that much. Pretty soon we started seeing each other. Our first date was at the Old Mill, and we clicked immediately. In spite of our different backgrounds — me a Catholic and she the daughter of a Baptist (hard to believe these things still mattered then) — we shared a sense of humour. With my move to Montreal in 1970 to take up the new posting with the Bank, we were engaged. We were married in 1971 in Toronto, and then moved our lives to Quebec.

In our partnership, we had a deal that if one of us wanted to go back to school, the other would support them while they did. She had graduated from high school in 1963 and gone directly to teacher's college, which you could do in those days. Her first job was teaching Grade 1 at Rosethorn Public School in Etobicoke in the west end of Toronto, where she was born and had grown up. But when I took the job in HR at head office in 1970 and we moved to Montreal, she couldn't get a job there immediately because she didn't have teaching credentials from the

Province of Quebec. She had applied to get a teaching certificate, but in the meantime she'd found an advertisement in the newspaper for an English teacher at a private Jewish girls' school in Montreal, the Beth Rivkah Academy for Girls.

So she applied for the job, she interviewed with the rabbi, and he hired her. The students were primarily young, French-speaking, Moroccan Jewish girls. It was a wonderful experience for Liz, except she didn't quite understand some of the nuances of this new environment. One of the things she did in her early days at the school was she posted a big map of Israel on the classroom wall to teach the kids all about it, given their background as Moroccan Jews, not Zionists. Next thing she knew, the rabbi came running into the classroom and tore it down. He said, "You don't understand." Unbeknownst to her, the school didn't support Zionism. Liz was just innocently trying to do her best to broaden the horizons of her students and teach them something about their Jewish heritage. Oops.

Six months later, she got a job offer from the Protestant School Board of Greater Montreal, as it was known then. She'd finally gotten her credentials and was able to start teaching in the public-school system. But she also started going to school at nights at Concordia, where she graduated with her major in English Literature, studying primarily contemporary Jewish-American writers such as Saul Bellow, Philip Roth, Bernard Malamud and Chaim Potok.

Later, according to our deal, Liz stopped teaching and went back to school, this time at McGill, earning a master's degree in Library Science. So now I had a librarian in the family. We spent a very happy ten years in Montreal, although Liz was not as happy as I was because she wasn't French-speaking. Despite being French Canadian on my mother's side, I was only moderately fluent in French, but I could get by.

Liz was the reader in the family. She was such an assiduous student when she got to Concordia, she just absorbed everything. She was a great student of people like Viktor Frankl, and his great book *Man's Search for Meaning*, as well as all the great poets and novelists. I had been an English student at university too, but I never had the patience to read every damn thing that was assigned for a course. Like the twelve books

I was supposed to read for a nineteenth-century novel course I took in second year. I took the fast track through those, skimming just enough to get by. But later, Liz would often say, "Tony, you have to read this novel," whether it was Jane Austen or one of the Brontës. And I would selectively read whatever Liz told me was important for me to read. It wasn't until much later that I gained a true appreciation for that course. My literary education was mostly *ex post facto*, all thanks to Liz.

When she went on to get her master's degree, she was still constantly reading. On the top shelves of my library is a collection of biographies, which is really *Liz's* collection of biographies. Books about every prominent person you can think of — and she read them all. She was a great fan of the genre and upstairs in one of my closets, I've got more of them that couldn't fit in the library — her collection of biographies of artists, painters and sculptors. I'm not about to read them, but I'm not about to get rid of them either. It's such a wonderful collection.

With Liz's interest in the arts and literature, it wasn't a surprise that, when we returned to Toronto, she became president of the board of directors at the Tarragon Theatre in 1982. Tarragon was famous as a producer of original Canadian theatre and had encouraged well-known writers such as David French, Carol Bolt and Michel Tremblay. Registered as a not-for-profit, it was in financial trouble when Liz took the position. She immediately saw what the need was at the time: they desperately needed corporate sponsors to support the productions. She jumped right into the job and leaned on my contacts to line up the best sponsors. (She never overtly told me that, of course, but you know, I'm not dumb.) That gave her the door opener to deliver her dynamite sales pitch on the great work Tarragon was doing developing Canadian theatre and why it was so important to invest in it.

Liz was able to secure corporate sponsors for every single one of Tarragon's productions for something like five years in a row and became a close friend to Urjo Kareda, the artistic director from 1982–2001, and Mallory Gilbert, the general manager of the place who passed away in 2019. Then she started working with Joe Rotman and John Evans, who had been the president of U of T in the 1970s and was married to the sister of Bill Glassco, the founder (with his wife Jane) of the Tarragon Theatre. Joe and John knew that one of the principal scientists at Mount Sinai's research institute was a geneticist named Dr. Lou Siminovitch, a world-renowned academic and researcher; he was also a saint, a wonderful person and communicator. His wife, Elinore, had been a great lover of theatre and she'd written several plays herself before she passed away in 1995. Fast forward to 2000, and it was about to be Lou Siminovitch's eightieth birthday. Joe and John had the brilliant idea to invent the Siminovitch Prize in Theatre, to celebrate Lou's life and achievements on this milestone birthday and to honour the memory of Elinore.

At dinner one night with Joe Rotman and John Evans, Joe announced to Liz that she was going to be the project manager of this prize, responsible for putting the whole thing together — from scratch. This task involved not just planning the evening of celebration but creating and establishing the prize itself. Liz was unsure at first, it being such a big project, but she quickly threw herself into it.

She recruited Urjo from Tarragon to be the first chair of the jury, and it was her idea to segment the prize, establishing a three-year cycle that recognized a different specialty each time: one year it would be a director, the next a playwright or set designer and then an arts administrator or leader in the theatre community. The prize would be $100,000, of which the winner was to designate $25,000 to someone to whom they were a mentor — a protégé who was an emerging talent in their profession. It was a huge prize for people in the theatre community at mid-career and those just coming up through the ranks. I began leaning on the Bank to sponsor the annual awards celebration, which would be at Hart House at U of T, with a reception afterwards in the Great Hall of Hart House.

Liz ran the Siminovitch Prize for ten years, pretending to hate every single minute of it. Every year I would hear, "I'm so tired of all this work. Why did I ever agree to do it and why did Joe Rotman push me into this?" But she truly loved it, and was Miss Magic, doing such wonderful work. Of course, the finances of the prize were a challenge, as they always are in fundraising of any kind. I kept saying to Rotman, "Joe, this is a limited amount of money, $100,000 a year. Unless you get this thing endowed and put in place a source of ongoing funding, it's going to run out of money in about eight years, then what are you going to do?" It all became very real and tangible when we put together the money.

Then, in 2012, our world was turned upside down. Liz was diagnosed with myelofibrosis, the rarest and the most virulent of the three forms of a class of diseases called myeloproliferative neoplasms. When Liz became sick we knew very little about the cause or the prognosis. It's so rare it's what I call an orphan disease; there are maybe 1,300 cases a year in Canada, and only about 13,000 in all of the U.S. Essentially, this is a rare type of bone marrow cancer that stops your body's generation of red blood cells.

We really had had little indication prior to this of something being wrong, though we did realize in retrospect that when we'd been in Paris in September of the previous year, Liz had been more fatigued than usual. Walking along the rue du Faubourg Saint-Honoré in 2010, she was getting out of breath and, as I thought about it later, this was happening more and more often. At first I thought it might be associated with smoking. Liz had quit smoking when we moved to England in 1984, but she had been a chronic smoker for years before that and had always had lung-related problems. But her smoking had nothing to do with the disease — it was genetic. We learned after her diagnosis that it was because she didn't have enough red blood cells.

It was only a matter of time before her myelofibrosis would show up and the only reason we discovered it when we did was thanks to a regular checkup. As a BMO executive, I was lucky to have a comprehensive benefits package and, fortunately, we were customers of Medcan, a company that provides health and wellness support to organizations and individuals. We didn't get just an annual checkup there; they put us through a complete head-to-toe evaluation every year — a comprehensive six-hour health assessment to take us through absolutely everything. It was a wonderful perk, actually. It was after Liz went for her annual appointment in 2012 that we got the news.

Bob Francis, a medical doctor who founded Medcan in 1987 and a good friend, called her up himself and told her she had to have a blood transfusion the next day. That's how bad it was. Her hemoglobin was down to 64; it should have been 120. Liz replied, "Gee, Bob, how about if I go next week, because Tony and I are going to Stratford this weekend?"

"No Liz, you've already got the appointment. It's at eight o'clock in the morning."

We recognized immediately that we were dealing with something serious. Liz dutifully went for the transfusion at St. Michael's Hospital the next day and the hematologist at the time, Dr. Dale Dotton, said, "Liz, I think you have myeloproliferative neoplasm. I'm not 100 percent certain, but I'm going to refer you to a doctor at Princess Margaret, Dr. Vikas Gupta, who really knows what this stuff is all about." Dr. Dotton was a brilliant doctor himself, but he said, "You've got to see the guy who really knows it."

In the meantime, I did some research of my own. I went to see Dr. Michael Baker, who was the head of medicine at University Health Network at Toronto General Hospital. He was also a hematologist, a very famous doctor and a close friend of Liz's. He advised, "Tony you've got to go see Vikas Gupta. There are only five guys in North America who know anything about this class of disease, and he's one of them."

So we did, and he got her into a regimen where she was going for a transfusion once a month, and then she'd be okay for a while. Still, we knew the odds. We were willing to try anything, no matter how unusual it seemed. One of our Jewish friends got Liz to go and see a rabbi in upstate New York, an area heavily populated by Orthodox Jews. The rabbi was an older guy, had been through the Holocaust and spoke only Yiddish. He prayed, and Liz had to sit beside me; he wasn't allowed to touch her, because she was a woman. I had to put my hand on his shoulder and hers at the same time, and so I was the connection. I was the link.

No matter what we tried — everything from medical treatments to spiritual healing — the disease got progressively worse and Liz developed severe diverticulitis at one point. It's a side effect of the myelofibrosis and caused her crippling abdominal pain. It got so bad she couldn't leave the house to see the doctor. I am eternally grateful for what Bob Francis did then. He would have two nurses from Medcan do house calls instead — one to do the ECG, and the other, a blood-transfusion and injection specialist, would come up to the apartment once a month and take care of everything she needed. And sometimes Bob would even come himself.

On one occasion, Liz was suffering severe abdominal pain and Bob came to take a look at her. "I don't like this," he said. "Her abdomen is distended and hard. We've got to get her into the hospital." He called ahead to the hospital, and we all went as quickly as possible. After we got there, she'd been lying in the hallway on a gurney for some time. Bob said, "She needs fluids, and she needs them now." He thought they were too slow off the mark. And so he went directly to the nursing station, and said, "Where's the on-call intern?"

They said, "He's down the hall."

Bob barked, "Well get his ass over here right now."

Bob started running the place, pretty much taking over the emergency department. Bob has two modes, one of which is Bob the Nice Guy, the other is Bob the Demon — and you don't want to get on that side. He was giving orders: "Get five doctors over here! Now!" And then Dr. Gupta arrived on the scene as well. Now there were two doctors running the place. It pissed everybody off, but Liz was extremely ill at this point. She was in the final stages of this terrible disease. It was desperate.

Dr. Gupta was amazing. He was an oncologist and hematologist at Princess Margaret Hospital, but they couldn't give him the time or funding to deal with this class of disease. As a rare orphan disease, it wasn't anywhere near as high on their priority list as "the biggies," the more common forms of cancer, so there was no money from the foundation for research and treatment. Anything Dr. Gupta did for his patients with this disease he virtually had to do in his own spare time. That included looking after Liz, his clinic and his other patients. He was very upfront with us. He took me aside and said, "Tony, it's now gotten to the phase where her white blood cell count is dropping. That means it's kicked into AML — acute myeloid leukemia. She's very close to not coming back. Should we talk to Liz?"

Yes. So we went into her room together, and he told her. Liz knew. She had always been very stoic and wouldn't ever let on to me if she was in distress or pain. She wasn't a complainer, and I think she was trying to protect me, in a way, from the reality of her disease, so I could stay focused at work. I wish at times I had been more aware of everything she had been going through, because I could have been more supportive if I had known what rough shape she was in. She was very weak. Liz and I had a private conversation, and I said, "You know, Liz . . . Gupta has been doing this out of his own pocket and there are other people that suffer from this. I think we should seriously think about putting a program in place to help him institutionalize this support."

She said, "You're right, Tony. I totally agree with that."

Liz died on June 22, 2014. As per her wish, we ponied up $2.4 million to allow Dr. Gupta to institutionalize research for myelofibrosis and the related forms of myeloproliferative neoplasms. I recently renewed this funding commitment, and he's now got a staff of seven, including three doctors and two researchers, and he's supporting other people across the country remotely. So, a doctor in Brandon, Manitoba, who has a patient with one of these diseases and doesn't know what to do about it, can connect with Dr. Gupta and his team online using Skype, for example, consult with him, and Dr. Gupta can advise them on treatment regimens and so on.

Dr. Gupta still sits down with me every six months to review the program and how they spent their money. Once he said to me, "Tony, you've got to name it the Elizabeth and Tony Comper Program." I said I didn't need the recognition, but he explained the way funding works. It wasn't about the recognition itself; unless we locked up the funds in a designated program, we were at risk of them going to other programs. So I said okay.

Now the program is up and running, and the funding is stable and secure, Dr. Gupta and his team are doing some very interesting research. He is an internationally recognized specialist in this area and has built up a tissue database of all the patients that have this rare disease. He and his fellow researchers are hot on the trail of identifying the markers of the disease in other patients and discovering what triggers acute myeloid leukemia in patients with myeloproliferative neoplasms.

So the work goes on. And if something good can come out of Liz's experience then it will be a tribute to her and her generosity in funding Dr. Gupta's work.

TONY'S TAKEAWAY

The lesson of Liz's life is that every successful person is a product of personal growth and a community of voices. But also, one person did make a difference. Don't be transfixed by only the people you see. Appreciate the people who underpin success from offstage.

CHAPTER 25

Signing Off: Fast Forward to Tomorrow

He who repeats a tale after a man,
Is bound to say, as nearly as he can,
Each single word, if he remembers it,
However rudely spoken or unfit,
Or else the tale he tells will be untrue,
The things invented and the phrases new.
— GEOFFREY CHAUCER, *The Canterbury Tales*

Liz had some memorable words for me on the day I retired. I quote them all the time, and everyone laughs. She said to me, "Now, Tony, I love you dearly, and I married you for life and everything else. But I didn't marry you for lunch. Now, get the hell out of here. You're not going to hang around here, you know!"

When the time came for me to leave the CEO position at BMO in 2007, I didn't have a long-term plan for what would come next. I know that might seem a little odd for me — the planner, the detail guy, the catastrophizer — not to worry over and wonder what the future might hold. But I was so focused on doing the job right up until the end that it really hadn't occurred to me.

Some people asked me how it would feel to be just another guy after a long career in leadership in the Bank. But I didn't think of my retirement that way; to me, it was just like having another day at the office. In all my forty years at BMO and in all the roles I held there, I'd never thought much about the next job. I'd never thought about the end of the current job. I'd always just thought, "What do I have to do tomorrow morning at eight o'clock?" That's just who I am. Old habits die hard. And as the old adage goes, a long journey starts with the first step.

An interesting thing about Bank of Montreal — and I think it says something about our approach to corporate governance — is that we've developed a rule that the retirement age of the CEO is sixty-two years of age, done. There's never any discretion. You can't be like FDR and ask for four terms. I don't know how far back this policy goes, but it has certainly been in effect for some time, probably as far back as Bill Mulholland, but maybe also to Fred McNeil and before him Arnold Hart.

Why sixty-two specifically as a retirement age for the CEO, as opposed to the more common age of sixty-five? It probably has something to do with years of service. Most executives in the Bank would have been long-serving employees by the time they hit their sixties. Take forty years of employment from age sixty-two and you land on twenty-two years of age — which is the average age of people starting at the Bank and working their way up. For whatever reason, sixty-two is the number for our purposes at the Bank. The Bank may have figured by the time you've done thirty-five to forty years of service, you deserve to hang up the skates.

Matt Barrett had a philosophy that also carries some weight. He believed that when you come to any top job — as chairman of the company, or CEO of a bank, or prime minister — you bring to the game a certain amount of intellectual capital and you start to spend it. It's not really renewable — you bring your own philosophy, your own thinking, your own approach and you pour them into the task of leadership. Like a Leyden jar in physics that stores up energy for future use, you spend this intellectual capital over a period of time, and Matt thought it lasted about ten years maximum. You're not going to reinvent your whole way of thinking about the world and what you should accomplish after that point.

That's when you should leave. And that's what Matt did in 1999 (although he was younger than sixty-two when his ten years as CEO were up). When I retired at sixty-two, Bill Downe took over. Ten years later he passed the baton to Darryl White, the current CEO. That emptying of the Leyden jar seems to tie neatly to roughly ten years in the job and/or to sixty-two years of age for most of the guys who have come up through the system in our Bank in recent years. Maybe they got the timing right without even knowing it.

The Bank's policy of mandatory retirement for CEOs at age sixty-two not only helps to ensure that the person in the top job is at the top of their game, but it also helps in managing the transition and the expectations of the entire organization. Everybody within the Bank knows what the rules are. Because we know that the CEO is leaving at sixty-two and can't try to hang on for four more years, there's no room for playing politics and undercutting that person, which does tend to go on in a lot of organizations that don't have a similar age limit. We know exactly what the date is, and what's going to happen. The board also has a predictable timeframe in which to think about the likely successors and all the usual questions about transitioning leaders, such as, "Is it going to be an internal candidate, or do we have to look outside?"

And when you're in the job, you know that's the end point. You don't have to spend a lot of time worrying and wondering, "Gee, what am I going to do if they ask me to hang around till I'm sixty-five or sixty-seven?" Or, "What if the Bank's in trouble and they needed some help?" Of course, you can always opt to retire before age sixty-two, but with a clear limit, there are fewer distracting questions about your future and you're able to concentrate on running the bank today, for what's best at the time.

Capping the age of the CEO is also good for younger people in an organization. It would discourage them if they thought that the person on top might be there until they're seventy-five and there would be no possibility of spots opening up for them. With an age limit in place for the CEO, aspiring leaders know there's a potential path to the C-suite as well as a timeline for getting there. They can say, "I know what the timing is for the CEO position, so therefore I've got to really fire my jets and score a few goals between now and then." Nor do you risk losing those same aspiring leaders when they choose to leave the organization in search of career advancement because they think, "This old fart's going to hold on until he's seventy." The politics of succession just simply evaporates, which I think is excellent.

Besides, some people had said nice things about me when I left, and why ruin that? I especially liked this from David Olive of the *Toronto Star*: "In our view, [Tony] Comper's success in more than doubling BMO's market cap, to almost $35 billion by the end of fiscal 2006, in an eight-year tenure capped by last year's record profit of $2.7 billion, deserves a tip of the hat. That's not including Comper's outstanding role as community builder in Toronto; or all the Enron Corp. and other potholes Comper managed to sidestep that his peers . . . stepped into. You can manage our money anytime, Tony."

Thank you, David. Very kind. And while this is not a book to recite statistics, let me say that I'm proud of the numbers that show the growth of the Bank over the years of my career and even until the present day. (As Warren Buffett said, "Only when the tide goes out do you discover who's been swimming naked.") While numbers aren't the final arbiter of success, they do give satisfaction to an old banker. As I said in the introduction, the three pillars that have made BMO a success are risk management, diversification and productivity. And I like to believe these results speak to that commitment.

I'm proud of the words on my citation that I received from the Board of Governors upon my retirement, which reads, in part: "Upon being named Chief Executive Officer in 1999, Mr. Comper led the single largest business transformation in BMO history, with the result that net income more than doubled from 1999–2006, during which time shareholders earned an average annual total return of 17.3 percent as he implemented a focused and disciplined North American growth strategy, expanded our Harris growth strategy in the U.S., [and] strengthened BMO's leadership in credit risk management, commercial and wealth management . . ."

Many people have asked me why I didn't remain on BMO's board of directors to keep my hand in. And I always say, the last thing I'd ever want to do is stay on the board and look over the shoulder of the new CEOs. In fact, I think it's really unwise for the retired CEO to hang around like a bad smell and intimidate the board and the new guy. It's important to know when to move on and to move on completely.

It's not that I completely disappeared. The next CEO, Bill Downe, was closely associated with BMO Financial Group and BMO Capital

Markets, and a lot of the centre of gravity of that business was shifting to the United States. He was spending a lot of his time in Chicago. In fact, that's where he had been for much of his career. So, even after I retired, he would routinely ask me to do customer events and other official duties back at the home office in Toronto.

I have kept an office there till recently, because I still do those sorts of ancillary, not particularly important, jobs. Plus, they asked me to stay on and be chair of the Art and Archives Committee. (We are also publishing an official history of the Bank written by Dr. Laurence Mussio.) So although I now have an office nearer my home, I'm still occasionally around First Canadian Place, with my own office on the sixty-eighth floor. I keep out of the way of the everyday leadership. It was more of a soft landing for me, if I can characterize it that way, as opposed to carrying my box of pencils out the door and winding up on the windy corner of King and Bay.

After structuring my life around my career at BMO for forty-three years, I didn't want to be totally at sixes and sevens. It's tough all of a sudden to take that framework and structure away and adlib it. Suddenly, "What am I going to do tomorrow?" took on a whole new meaning. I'm not the kind to sit around and watch TV or go down to Timmy's to hang around and read the papers. I'll still be at the Maple Leafs and Raptors games. I'll still head to Stratford to see the latest gems on offer. I'll be at the AGO and McMichael to see the latest exhibits. And yes, I'll be noodling around St. Michael's College to indulge my thirst for learning in medieval studies.

Think of this, not as goodbye, but till we meet again.

TONY'S TAKEAWAY

Knowing when to leave is an art form that few appreciate. My policy has always been *festina lente*: make haste slowly. And I suspect as long as there are great books and good friends, that's the way it will continue to be.

ACKNOWLEDGEMENTS

From Tony:

The Tale of the Memoir: After I retired, I often reflected on my over forty years (plus an additional six years of part-time!) with the Bank. I thought about writing about my experiences for the benefit of my colleagues, present and to follow, perhaps providing some useful insights, which informed any success I achieved.

I didn't want it to be a "when Tony was three" memoir, but a recounting of my diverse experiences. I mulled this over with my dear friend Carol. We'd known each other for almost forty years, each of us BMO colleagues and collaborators in our early days with the Bank. She is a remarkable person with many diverse skills and talents, a wonderful personality and amazing interpersonal skills; kindness personified! We share many interests from literature to sports. She has a particular passion for literature with a special love of the classics: Tolstoy, Dickens, D.H. Lawrence, Vonnegut and Greene. She has been a perfect companion to help thinking about the structure of the memoir and how to tell "my story." She was instrumental and persuasive in convincing me to embark on the project, dreamed up the structure and theme for it, and provided endless advice and encouragement throughout its development. What good fortune for me!

She often mentioned a friend from her college days, now an accomplished author, but we had never met. I finally met Bruce Dowbiggin in person for the first time in the summer of 2017 but felt that I had known him for years, as Carol would mention her accomplished friend often in discussion. Carol arranged for us to meet at a Blue Jays ball game, and Bruce and I immediately became friends. Shortly after our first meeting, I broached the subject of his helping me with a memoir, and he readily agreed.

We then searched for a way to bring my collection of stories together. The common theme was the interrelated but different perspectives on what I had learned over a long career, like the facets of a cut stone, or in music, a *leitmotif*. One day, mulling this over with Carol, she reminded me that I had studied Chaucer in graduate school. Bruce and I concluded that *The Canterbury Tales* were a perfect analogue to the collection of stories in my memoir. Bruce is a thoughtful intellectual, an accomplished author of seven (soon to be nine) books, an award-winning TV commentator, an economic conservative as am I, and a talented writer who routinely turned my inelegant verbosity into lucid prose. Although decisive in "business mode," he belies a sensitivity befitting the talented poet that he is. I am lucky to count him a close friend, and I thank Carol for bringing us together. And I thank both of them for their friendship and support.

There is, as Thomas Aquinas said, nothing on this earth more to be prized than true friendship.

Throughout my career, I was blessed to meet and count as friends, and in some cases colleagues, a truly sparkling group of accomplished individuals who supported me with their friendship and advice throughout the years, and they remain dear friends to this day. Of course, Nancy Greco, who was instrumental in producing the countless versions of the memoir and coordinating the countless meetings, calls and other arrangements. She frequently had nightmares of three-ring binders marching towards her, each armed with an electronic three-hole punch!

For everyone who shared their stories, anecdotes and reminiscences in the Foreword and Voices that appear in these pages, I can't thank them enough for everything they have been to me and to my beloved Liz over the years.

I'd also like to acknowledge several friends and associates who have made an enormous contribution with their help and advice. Dr. Laurence Mussio, author of *Whom Fortune Favours: The Bank of Montreal and the*

Ascent of Canadian Banking, who vetted the manuscript more than twice for historical and other facts. Bruce, of course, my long-suffering alchemist who turned my babbling into coherent narrative.

Austin Adams, a fellow board member at Spectra Energy who was CIO at major U.S. banks, and who shared insights into the challenges of this role, one we shared. Karen Milner, our editor, who made this a better book. Miranda Hubbs, who educated me in the contemporary corporate focus on E.S.A. and other matters on the current agenda of CEOs. Danaka Bailey, who provided a younger generation perspective on many of the chapters. Tom Flynn and his colleague Sukhwinder Singh for validating financial data. Thanks as well to Yuula Benivolski for permission to use her striking cover photo.

Darryl White, who made an initial commitment to support my endeavour by agreeing to acquire copies for the Bank and our colleagues. Thank you, one and all.

From Bruce:

I first met Tony at his seats in the Rogers Centre for a Toronto Blue Jays game. I soon discovered that he's as much at home watching a ballgame as he was at handling a BMO board of directors meeting. It took us about twenty minutes to realize all the links we shared — U of T grads, products of Catholic education, sports fans, a history at Tarragon Theatre with Urjo Kareda, intellectual curiosity about the arcane, ties to Western Canada, etc. And with a handshake we were committed to *Personal Account.*

Having a front-row seat for some of the most impactful financial stories of the past fifty years has been a privilege. I remain grateful that Tony chose me to help him tell the story of his extraordinary life and career. There were many capable business journalists who'd have been happy to cooperate with him. But his hunch on a sports journalist who's also been a playwright, a poet and a published author himself is pure Tony. He identifies a skillset he wants, he tells you what he requires and, unless you hear otherwise, he trusts you to finish the task. And while there were times when I felt guilty about the demanding writing process I put him though, Tony was a trooper who wanted only the best book we could create.

Work on this project would never have advanced a foot without the tender ministrations of my long-time friend — and Comper colleague at BMO — Carol Thomson. I also wish to thank Tony's home team — Nancy and Enzo Greco — for their help and cooperation in keeping the boss's recollections flowing.

At ECW, Jennifer Smith has been nothing but supportive as she guided this project to completion. Our editor Karen Milner improved the manuscript in so many smart ways, and we are grateful for her experienced eye. So, too, Jen Hale for her patience and attention to grammatical detail. The rest of the ECW production and promotion staff — Emily Ferko, Jessica Albert, Susannah Ames — have also been great during a turbulent time of COVID-19 and self-isolation. Thanks again to David Caron and Michael Holmes for having faith in the project.

On a personal note, my own family has increased while we worked on the book. So I dedicate my sliver of the work to Oliver and Emmeline Dowbiggin — and the prospect of more grandchildren to discover Grandpa's books in the future.

INDEX

Note: TC is an abbreviation of Tony Comper.